GLOBAL INEQUALITY

GLOBAL INEQUALITY

Kenneth McGill

ANTHROPOLOGICAL INSIGHTS

UNIVERSITY OF TORONTO PRESS

Library and Archives Canada Cataloguing in Publication
McGill, Kenneth, 1973–, author
Global inequality / Kenneth McGill.
Includes bibliographical references and index.
Issued in print and electronic formats.

ISBN 978-1-4426-3452-7 (hardback).—ISBN 978-1-4426-3451-0 (paperback).
—ISBN 978-1-4426-3454-1 (pdf).—ISBN 978-1-4426-3453-4 (html).

1. Equality. 2. Ethnology—Case studies. I. Title.

HM821.M35 2016   305   C2015-907496-7
                                      C2015-907497-5

We welcome comments and suggestions regarding any aspect of our publications—
please feel free to contact us at news@utphighereducation.com or visit our Internet
site at www.utppublishing.com.

North America   UK, Ireland, and continental Europe
5201 Dufferin Street   NBN International
North York, Ontario, Canada, M3H 5T8   Estover Road, Plymouth, PL6 7PY, UK

                                       ORDERS PHONE: 44 (0) 1752 202301
2250 Military Road   ORDERS FAX: 44 (0) 1752 202333
Tonawanda, New York, USA, 14150   ORDERS E-MAIL:
                                       enquiries@nbninternational.com

ORDERS PHONE: 1-800-565-9523
ORDERS FAX: 1-800-221-9985
ORDERS E-MAIL: utpbooks@utpress.utoronto.ca

Every effort has been made to contact copyright holders; in the event of an error or
omission, please notify the publisher.

The University of Toronto Press acknowledges the financial support for its
publishing activities of the Government of Canada through the Canada Book Fund.

Printed in the United States of America.
Cover design: Grace Cheong.

CONTENTS

FIGURES

PREFACE

This book is a cross between an ordinary textbook and a work of scholarly research. It is written for undergraduates and broadly addresses the topic of inequality from the perspective of a cultural anthropologist.

Why write a book of this sort? I hope that most readers can guess the weaknesses of traditional textbooks, which present knowledge ready-made and neatly packaged. As I argue in the next chapter, it is all but inevitable that inequality must be addressed from a personal point of view. This is particularly the case with global inequality. As I also argue further below, our best understanding of globalization centers on actual relationships between people, rather than on abstract and impersonal judgments of completely distinct societies or cultures. My understanding of global inequality cannot be given to you; instead, you must find your own.

There are also limits to traditional scholarly research. Ideas arrived at by cultural anthropologists are normally couched in an academic rhetoric, and they moreover tend to be bound to highly detailed case studies. When anthropologists do seek to synthesize a variety of findings from different sources, what they usually end up with are abstract theories rather than specific conclusions. By contrast, my goal in this book is to make ethnographic fieldwork less abstract and more immediately meaningful.

In this vein, it should be pointed out that this book does not involve any new research. I mostly present the work of other ethnographers, and I mostly do so at some length. Throughout, my goal is to introduce novel ideas of global inequality based on previously available research. This book should not be viewed as a survey of different forms of inequality in the world, or even a review of the scholarly literature on globalization and inequality. Rather, it is my attempt to define what it means to talk about global inequality today from the perspective of a cultural anthropologist.

I am well aware that economic inequality has been a topic of growing concern in both the United States and Canada. It must be stated, however, that popular debates about inequality in these countries have been needlessly narrow and parochial. The fact of the matter is that we live in an extraordinarily unequal world. Addressing inequality within rich countries is important, but it is equally important that we think about inequality as it exists *across* national boundaries. I do not suggest that our concern for within-nation inequality should simply be forgotten (indeed, a good part of this book is dedicated specifically to that topic). Instead, I call on the readers of this volume to be sophisticated enough to contemplate inequality on multiple scales and in numerous contexts, including both national and transnational ones.

Only a few small points remain to be made. First, this book involves several estimations of global economic facts, such as the median global income. These figures are presented in US dollars. Second, appendices can be found at the end of this book with suggestions for additional reading materials and films organized by book chapter, as well as study questions.

CHAPTER 1

INTRODUCTION: ANTHROPOLOGY AND INEQUALITY

Global inequality matters.

This proposition has two important parts: First, that inequality matters. Second, that it is important to examine inequality from a global perspective.

ˎ Let me begin with the notion that inequality matters. People define themselves in relation to one another. This means that the inequalities that exist between us are bound to affect who we actually are. In this sense, inequality matters because it is part of the relationships that define us. Even in those moments when inequality seems clearly justifiable, it remains a problem. To be unequal to someone else is to be different from them in a way that truly matters. ˗

The second key proposition of this book is that it is important for us to consider inequality in a global framework. There are, and always will be, local contexts that are crucial for the definition of equality and inequality. I am not in the least suggesting that we ignore these contexts. However, I would also like to suggest that there are no local contexts that can ever completely contain our concerns about inequality. If inequality is indeed about relationships, then we must recognize that relationships are never strictly bound to a single place. The ongoing growth of global relationships points very directly toward the increasing importance of global inequality.

We might say that global thinking and relational thinking go together. If we begin by looking at relationships in a local context, our methods are bound, at the very least, to draw our attention toward those relationships that extend beyond this context. Conversely, beginning with a global context requires us to think about relationships as the means by which this context is constituted across specific locations. And as one scholar after another has indeed affirmed, it is relationships that matter to our notion of globalization. The sociologist David Held and his coauthors (1999: 14) have defined globalization as the "widening, deepening and speeding up of global interconnection." The political scientist Manfred Steger (2003: 1) has similarly referred to "the increasingly interdependent nature of social life on our planet." Arjun Appadurai (1996: 27), an anthropologist widely read outside the discipline, defines globalization as involving "an interactive system that is strikingly new." The emphasis in each of these cases is on interconnection, interdependence, and interaction—in other words, on the sorts of relationships that exist on a planetary scale.

Thinking about Inequality

When most people consider inequality, their thoughts turn first to the economic differences that constitute wealth and poverty. As I describe in Chapter 3, there are any number of statistics that point rather urgently to global economic inequality as a major concern. Nevertheless, it is important to point out that inequality is not a strictly economic phenomenon. Inequality occurs in all kinds of forms—people can be unequal with regards to political power as well as economic wealth; with respect to their gender, ethnic identity, or sexuality; strictly in terms of their social status; and within all manner of schools, workplaces, cities, nations, or even individual homes.

But regardless of its type or location, inequality is inevitably something that must be experienced to exist. As the anthropologist Lloyd Fallers (1973: 5) argued some 40 years ago, even the most apparently "objective inequalities" can be understood only "in the context of their *meaning* to those involved." Because they are most easily measured, economic inequalities lend themselves to more objective analysis. However, it is the experience of inequality—and not its measurement—that is our ultimate concern. Inequality matters in personal, subjective ways.

The fact that inequality has a specifically subjective dimension should not prevent us from attempting to formulate a working definition of the term. To begin with, someone concerned with inequality is not merely concerned with the fact that people are different, or even that they are located at different positions within the same society. Rather, inequality refers to some sort of difference in status, wealth, or power that is to the benefit of one person or group and to the detriment of another. Inequality is about differences in the things that people value and not simply differences between people per se.

A related point is that there is no single form of equality or inequality that trumps all others. I have already mentioned that most people associate the notion of inequality with specifically economic inequalities. A related notion is that economic inequality is justifiable (at least within certain bounds), while political life demands a stricter adherence to equal rights and recognition.

As I argue at more length in Chapter 5, political equality is frequently held up as a crucial aspect of national belonging. In today's world, many more people are dedicated to a notion of equal rights than are to one of equal wealth. Ultimately, however, political and economic forms of inequality are interdependent and cannot easily be separated. It is impossible to define an egalitarian political regime that is insulated from other forms of inequality. Indeed, what would appear to be the case from certain ethnographic examples presented below is that meaningful political equality is almost impossible to achieve in the face of large disparities in economic wealth.

It is not merely economic and political inequality that are deeply inter-related. As we unwind individual ethnographic cases, what we find is that no single form of inequality ever occurs in isolation. Just as inequality cannot be fully contained in local contexts, so too can no single form of inequality ever be viewed in complete isolation. An important conclusion to draw from this—and once again, this is a point made by Fallers (1973: 29)—is the folly of viewing society in anything like simple "strati-graphic" terms. No society is neatly organized into a single hierarchical structure, with each person assigned to a clear "level" or position in that hierarchy. It is, of course, true that hierarchies exist and even that they can be deeply entrenched. Nevertheless, it is crucial for us to understand that inequality is something that *happens* in a complex and shifting world, rather than something that *simply exists* by virtue of a fixed social structure.

While many other interesting and worthwhile theoretical claims could be made here, it is precisely the point of an anthropological analysis that we skip strictly theoretical arguments in favor of grounded interpreta-tions of specific cases. For this reason, much of the book you are reading is given over to discussions of the work of particular ethnographers. As I discovered in the course of researching this book, almost every eth-nography has something interesting to say about inequality. The decisions I have made to include this or that ethnography have been based largely on the immediate accessibility of the scholarship in question to a broad audience, as well as that particular ethnography's usefulness in highlighting one or another part of my argument. For students who have taken more than one cultural or linguistic anthropology course, it might be interesting to look back at previously encountered ethnographies and consider how they reflect on the topic of inequality. Further readings can also be found in the Appendix 1 at the end of the book.

Anthropology between Global and Local

For anthropologists, a key point of interest involves the way that concerns about global relationships can be integrated into ethnographic fieldwork taking place on the local level. Over the past few decades, anthropologists have slowly come to grapple with this difficulty. An excellent example comes from the French anthropologist Marc Augé who summarizes anthropology's globalization predicament quite nicely:

> Traditionally, ethnography is the study of social relations within a narrow group defined by their geographical, historical and political context. But today context is always planetary … This puts into question the distinction between ethnography, as local observation, and anthropology, as a general and comparative point of view. Today, every ethnography must be an anthropology. (Augé 2013: 5)

4

Globalization challenges us not only to think on a broader scale, but also to integrate our specific concerns into a new kind of general intellectual framework, one which Augé simply and cleverly labels *anthropology*.

To expand on Augé's argument, I would make the case that understanding inequality is crucial to the establishment of this sort of specifically anthropological framework. The notion that every ethnography must address the "planetary" context also implies, at least for me, that every ethnography must be relevant, in at least some way, to the topic of inequality. Inequality is an inescapable feature of global relationships, and insofar as we might wish to understand how these global relationships affect local contexts, we must be willing to address inequality on a consistent basis. There are, of course, many different topics that matter to anthropological research. What I am suggesting here is that inequality cuts across these different topics—and, moreover, that examining inequality allows us to strengthen the "general and comparative point of view" required of today's ethnographic research.

Of course, it is still the case that most ethnographers establish their academic credentials by performing an ethnography that sticks to the "facts on the ground" within a particular fieldsite. As it happens, I think this is a good thing. The texture that locally engaged ethnographers bring to their scholarship is often the very thing that allows us to engage with the world in a way that is both personally compelling and intellectually rigorous. In this book, these local contexts include squatter settlements in Brazil, factories in China, and high schools in the United States. These sorts of local contexts will not disappear merely because new sorts of global relationships are being established. On the contrary, they will be reconsidered repeatedly as we consider inequality as a defining global condition.

Inequality and Global Systems

Given the sort of orientation to ethnographic fieldwork that I am suggesting, it makes sense that there are moments when we will want to consider the global context in and of itself. Particularly in this book, we will want to ask ourselves about the global context as one within which it is possible to perceive systematic inequality. To claim that global inequality has systematic aspects is not the same thing, of course, as claiming that there is a *single global system* that regulates the presence of inequality throughout the world. As the sociologist Sylvia Walby (2007) has emphasized, the very notion of globalization involves an irreducible complexity. This complexity is particularly important for the study of inequality, since multiple forms of inequality can coexist alongside one another without being commensurable or without resolving into one another. To borrow one of Walby's more succinct formulations (1986: 5), there is no "primary form of inequality."

With this warning in mind, a helpful way to begin to address the systematic aspects of global inequality is to consider specific institutions. We are surrounded by all manner of institutions that support the existence of inequality, and each of these institutions does indeed have its own systematic character. Perhaps most immediately notable in this regard are nation-states. The borders between nation-states wall off—sometimes quite literally—the residents of rich countries from the rest of the world. At the same time, most discussions about inequality remain discussions about inequality *within* nations. This has very much been the case in the United States in recent years, as the discourse surrounding the "99 per cent" versus the top "1 per cent" of income earners remains specifically centered on inequality within the country. The nation-state is therefore an important institutional actor in the maintenance of transnational inequality and, at the same time, a key lens through which inequality is understood.

Compared to the nation-state, a global institution that is much less readily apparent is the one we might refer to as *global patriarchy*. No one would deny the fact that Canada or the United States exists and that there are global inequalities between these countries and others such as Haiti or Namibia. However, to maintain that there exists a form of global inequality between men and women is to invite all manner of questions and objections. Except in very local instances, there is no official representative organization of different genders. In this sense, global patriarchy does not have an obvious institutional locus. This is in spite of the fact that, as one influential anthropologist has argued (Ortner 1974: 67), "The secondary status of woman in society is one of the true universals, a pan-cultural fact." In a globalizing world, however, it is not the clear institutional organization of patriarchy that matters so much as its prevalence. As I attempt to specify in Chapter 4, the prevalence of patriarchal social relations across widespread locales implies a growing network of social relations dominated by men. This emergent global patriarchy exists in spite of certain feminist advances that have occurred during recent decades, particularly in rich countries. To borrow the formulation of the sociologist Arlie Hochschild and the journalist Barbara Ehrenreich, what we increasingly find is a secondary status for women specifically as *global subjects*. While gender identities are fluid and vary a great deal from place to place, there is also an axis of differentiation between men and women that increasingly operates on a global scale. Although it remains largely underappreciated within anthropology, scholars of globalization are increasingly aware of this fact.

Although limitations on space do not allow for a close examination of all of them, there are other sorts of inequalities that we might want to consider as having an increasingly global and systematic character. It seems quite clear, for example, that ethnic discrimination and discrimination against queer people are forms of inequality that operate on an increasingly global scale. Again, in Chapter 4, I consider the way in which homophobia and Islamophobia have become entangled within certain discussions of the Israeli-Palestinian conflict. Referring somewhat more narrowly to discrimination against queer people, however, the anthropologist Don Kulick (2009) has very succinctly asked whether there can be an "anthropology of homophobia" across anthropological fieldsites—and even more succinctly answered yes. Again, the facts on the ground regarding sexual practice, sexual orientation, and sexual identity are enormously variable. Kulick (2009: 22) is therefore careful to avoid taking homophobia as an "unproblematic, transcultural given." Nonetheless, what his argument makes clear is that we face a world today in which local ideas about sex and sexuality are increasingly interrelated and, therefore, in which genuinely global forms of both homophobia and sexual equality can emerge.[1]

It is very much possible to make an argument that economic inequality is the most basic form of inequality and that capitalism provides that basic institutional framework for inequality in the world today. While I reject this argument as a crude reduction of the many forms of inequality that exist side by side and influence one another, I do recognize the remarkable way in which capitalist economic relationships both encourage economic inequality and, at the same time, fuel all manner of global integration. For centuries, capitalist economies have been associated with an ever-growing pool of wealth and a constant flow of technological innovation. This tendency toward expansion and innovation is the most important cause of the increasing global interconnectedness we see today. The growth of capitalist economies is realized in the form of a constant drive for new sources of materials, new pools of labor, and new consumer markets. The dynamics of capitalist growth, however, cannot be separated from its tendency to

---

1   In Appadurai's well-known terms, we encounter a world of what might be considered increasingly coherent "ethnoscapes" and, I would argue, "genderscapes" and "sexuality-scapes." It seems to me, apropos the subject matter of this book, that the sort of formless inequalities implied by these "-scape" terms are less than specific about the sorts of inequality and discrimination more clearly implied by terms such as *global patriarchy* and *global homophobia*.

cement inequality. Capitalist economies require workers who generate more wealth than they take home in wages. The excess generated by this arrangement accrues to capital investors as profits. Critics of capitalism, beginning with Karl Marx, have argued that this arrangement is not only unfair, but results in the gradually diminishing power and wealth of workers (see, for example, Marx 1891). Defenders of capitalism have responded that the division between wages and capital is an unavoidable prerequisite of economic growth under modern conditions and that attempts to redistribute wealth outside this division will necessarily fail (see, for example, Friedman 2009).

While disagreements about the precise nature and value of capitalism are rampant, few would disagree that economic inequality is a clear prerequisite for capitalist economic production. In the spirit of the argument established at the beginning of this chapter, I would therefore suggest that capitalism is a problem for ethnographers in the field and for anthropologists concerned about global inequality. Although this book is not intended to thoroughly describe capitalism from an ethnographic point of view, I will be returning at several points to discuss how we can view capitalist economic relationships in light of a more clearly grounded concern about economic inequality itself. In the next chapter, for example, I attempt to show how anthropologists have dealt with the topic of inequality in light of capitalism as a global economic system.

Anthropology and the Colonial Legacy

The historian George Stocking (1991: 4) has described how, since the 1970s, anthropologists have arrived at the "commonplace" notion that anthropology is "linked to Western colonialism." Colonialism was a brutally inegalitarian system, most often involving domination by force and even genocide at the hands of colonial conquerors. As the anthropologist Jean Jackson (2009) has recently documented, the genocide of indigenous people is, in fact, an ongoing phenomenon. Even amidst the brutality of colonialism, however, colonial administrators also had a compelling need to understand the people whom they conquered. The result was a close relationship between certain forms of colonial rule and certain forms of ethnographic knowledge. Many of the most important types of knowledge gained by colonial regimes did not come from academically trained social scientists, but rather from various missionaries, adventurers, traders, colonial officials, and the like. Nevertheless, there have been important debates about the complicity of academic anthropologists in colonial rule—for example, about the role of British academic anthropologists in directly "aiding and abetting" British colonial rule in Africa (Pels and Salemink 2000: 5). The anthropologist Nicholas B. Dirks (1997: 209) has made the particularly strong claim that "Indian anthropology was in fact born directly out of the colonial project of ruling India."

Today, there are two reasons to be concerned about the relationship between anthropology and colonialism. First, there is some case to be made that the very tools of ethnographic research are suspect. The notion that a particular group of people can be isolated to be studied reminds us of the way that colonial domination separated people into clearly divided, administrable units. Indeed, the very word "ethnography" would seem to indicate that what is being studied is a particular *ethnos*—a category whose very formulation suggests the presence of a stereotyped ethnic other. As any practicing anthropologist can attest, ethnography always runs the risk of presenting its subjects as stereotypes. To make this critique, it is not necessary to suggest that contemporary anthropologists are directly responsible for propagating ethnic stereotypes. Rather, it is only necessary to suggest that the very notion of submerging oneself into a local cultural context is dependent on the objectification of an ethnic other. It is no coincidence that fieldwork after World War II in the decolonized "new states" most clearly pushed anthropologists to confront a world of interconnected and creatively imagined, rather than isolated and primordially present, cultures (see Geertz 1963).

Although it is related to this first one, the second and more serious concern focuses more clearly on the legacy of colonialism for the world as a whole. The unequal world that we live in today has very much been shaped by the history of colonialism. The poor countries of the world are overwhelmingly those whose native populations were colonized, while the rich countries of the world are overwhelmingly those who did the colonizing. It is no coincidence, therefore, that many contemporary critics of global power relations refer to certain relationships between these countries as involving a form of "neo-colonialism." Our global present is very much rooted in the colonial past. Even if they were able to account for their discipline's role in colonial rule, contemporary anthropologists can hardly escape ongoing relevance of the colonial past.

The continued division between rich and poor countries has both political and economic aspects, which will be discussed in some more detail in the next chapter. For the moment, however, it is important to point out that publishing anthropologists not only are members of the academic establishment, but also belong to the wealthiest fraction of the global population. Most are employed at universities in the wealthiest countries and are, if not always wealthy in local terms, at least part of a very prosperous society. Most also travel from rich countries to poor countries to carry out their fieldwork. Even anthropologists whose fieldwork takes place in other rich countries (my own research, for example, occurs primarily in Germany) are most likely to study people who are poorer than themselves (my research, to continue the same example, centers on the lives of poor and unemployed people).

The moral quandaries of fieldwork in a world divided between rich and poor have been discussed by Clifford Geertz (1968), who argues that an emphasis on "thinking as a moral act" can allow ethnographers to be both removed from and engaged with the economic divisions that affect their research process. In more concrete terms, however, anthropologists are well advised to consider how the colonial legacy impacts the people they study. An excellent example of this can be found in the work of Elizabeth Povinelli (1998, 2002), who has argued that the particular form of settler colonialism that preceded the Australian nation-state serves to exclude indigenous Australian populations in a very particular way. Some readers will be aware of the legal doctrine of *terra nullius*, according to which British colonizers declared their right to occupy the ostensibly empty lands that were in fact occupied by indigenous Australians. A key tenet of this doctrine was that individual indigenous people could not own land and, thus, could not transact with settlers to sell that land. Among other things, the result of this doctrine was the loss of lands traditionally inhabited by indigenous Australians.

Povinelli argues, however, that the disadvantage of native people does not occur simply in the form of a one-time land grab. Eventually, the Australian state did shift to the formal recognition of individual indigenous Australians as rights-bearing subjects capable of owning individual plots of land. However, the result of this recognition was to undercut ongoing claims made by these people collectively, as members of larger social groups. The basis for indigenous land claims often depends on ritual practices and kinship ties, rather than on the clear assignment of ownership over a bounded tract. As Povinelli notes, the recognition of indigenous Australians as members of the nation results in their further disadvantage. When individual land claims are paramount, indigenous claims to the land are easy to discount. After having been initially disqualified in a formal way from recognition as landholders, indigenous Australians now have distinct difficulties in making the particular style of land claim that is appropriate to their cultural heritage.

This summary of Povinelli's work could be looked on as a capsule lesson in the limitations of formal legal equality. However, it can also be taken as evidence for the broader importance of historical context in ethnographic fieldwork. Indigenous land claims in Australia differ from other land claims because of the conditions under which indigenous people were incorporated into the nation as colonized people. Anthropologists who are attentive to this sort of colonial historical context will be better prepared to deal with present-day inequality.

Anthropology's Encounter with (In)equality
A frequent practice in cultural anthropology textbooks is to differentiate societies on a spectrum from those that are most egalitarian to those

that are most stratified. Indeed, there are even cases where human cultures are presented as strictly divided into those two groups. Here is an example:

> In previous chapters, we encountered societies in which everyone has equal access to resources, livelihood and respect. We also encountered societies in which access to resources, livelihood and respect is given more to some people than to others. The first type of system, based on principles of equality between members of communities, is called egalitarian. The second type, based on social, economic and political inequality, is called stratified. (Bonvillain 2010: 277)

The notion of a neat division between egalitarian and stratified societies has a long history in anthropology. In the 1930s, the famed British anthropologist E.E. Evans-Pritchard maintained that the Nuer people he studied (in present-day Sudan) were rather strictly egalitarian. Here is one of his most memorable attempts to characterize this state of affairs:

> That every Nuer considers himself as good as his neighbor is evident in their every movement. They strut about like lords of the earth, which, indeed, they consider themselves to be. There is no master and no servant in their society, but only equals who regard themselves as God's noblest creation. (Evans-Pritchard 1940: 182)

This passage was quoted years later by Susan McKinnon (2000), in her reappraisal of Nuer kinship practices and critique of Evans-Pritchard's scholarly conclusions. The basic thrust of McKinnon's argument is that Evans-Pritchard's characterization of Nuer society as a strictly egalitarian one constitutes a vast simplification.

In particular, Evans-Pritchard expounded a model of kinship in which each segment of a particular Nuer lineage was equal to all others. Working with Evans-Pritchard's own published materials, what McKinnon is able to show is that this model of kinship hinged on classifying all people who descended through a particular lineage as political equals in Nuer society at large, while insisting that differences in status were merely a matter of divisions within a particular family or ritual group. In other words, Evans-Pritchard is able to define Nuer society as egalitarian because he confines all its inegalitarian features to non-political contexts. McKinnon's reanalysis shows us that Evans-Pritchard had forced his Nuer research materials into a strict and untenable dichotomy between egalitarian and stratified societies, rather than attempting to engage with their full complexity.

Other ethnographers have made similar criticisms of Evans-Pritchard. Most prominently, Sharon Elaine Hutchinson (2000: 56) has argued that many ethnographers of Evans-Pritchard's generation were concerned with "'unity,' 'equilibrium,' and 'order,'" rather than the "points of confusion and disagreement" that exist within Nuer society. Hutchinson insists that there is no completely unified Nuer culture and that the local context under study cannot therefore be described as egalitarian in any clear-cut way. In reality, Nuer people disagree with one another about their shared practices and identities, and issues of equality and inequality are bound to be caught up in these disagreements.

Similar concerns could be raised about other distinctions made by anthropologists, especially within the subfield of political anthropology. An important example involves the traditional anthropological division between bands, tribes, chiefdoms, and states—also a staple of cultural anthropology textbooks.[2] These categories speak to an attempt to understand equality and inequality as something that emerges from a particular "type" or "stage" of human culture. It is certainly the case that there are connections to be made regarding, for example, the ways in which political centralization relates to the manifestation of inequality. It seems misplaced, however, to suggest that local cultural contexts can be strictly classified by the degrees of political centralization they evince and that this classification, moreover, can provide the basis for understanding local forms of inequality. Certainly these sorts of categories are impossible to maintain in a more global analysis, where political systems are interrelated across local contexts. Strict typological comparisons have all but disappeared from anthropological thinking and are now found only in certain textbooks.

The Production of Inequality: A Case Study

Anthropologists began to formulate a more nuanced approach to inequality in the 1970s. I have already mentioned the work of Lloyd Fallers as a case in point. Another landmark came in 1985, with the publication of Lisette Josephides's book entitled *The Production of Inequality: Gender and Exchange among the Kewa.* This book was generally well received as a contribution to economic anthropology and the anthropology of gender. My interest in Josephides's book, however, begins with its evocative title. At the core of Josephides's argument is the claim that *inequality is produced* by people, rather than simply occurring by some natural or accidental means. Throughout her ethnography, Josephides attempts to show how people make inequality by virtue of choices they make every day, and it is this "produced" connection between everyday life and inequality that I find so deeply important to my own anthropological concerns.

Of course, it is ironic that I am borrowing from Josephides to discuss specifically global forms of inequality, since her work involves an extremely

---

2   For a fairly typical use of these categories, originally formulated by the anthropologist Elman Service in 1962, see Kottak (2011: 185).

small group of people relatively isolated from the outside world. At the time of Josephides's research, the Kewa linguistic group comprised some 50,000 people, and her own fieldwork focused on only a small group of about 600 Kewa-speaking people in a handful of settlements scattered across a single river valley. As is frequently the case in this part of Papua New Guinea, the Kewa with whom Josephides lived were vocally dedicated to the notion of equality, but specifically among men. In the local idiom, "one man is as good as another" (Josephides 1985: 198). There are no official political offices among Kewa people, although there are "big men" who take it upon themselves to actively guide economic production and organize ritual feasts. Exchanges between men are understood to be strictly between equals and strictly involving goods of equal value. In general, the material lifestyles of even the most important big men and their families are not substantially different from those of anyone else.

12

This ideology of masculine equality coincides with a belief in the essential difference between men and women. The Kewa people in Josephides's study consistently point to basic differences between genders in character, temperament, moral strength, and the like. Women are frequently represented as "sojourners" who travel between their own families and those of their husbands, while men are typically referred to as "base men of the place"—that is, people fundamentally rooted in the place they live. In certain ways, women are still respected as equal persons; Josephides (1985: 140) reports that a "widely held belief is that all persons [i.e., both men and women] have intrinsic value and must be accorded a degree of respect and consideration." Still, Josephides argues that differences in women's and men's positions in the "prestige structure" of Kewa society help to guide how people evaluate and treat one another. "For a man to be called womanly denotes regression and deterioration. When a woman is accused of trying to be like a man she is ridiculed for aspiring so high" (133).

> In addition to these ideological features, Kewa society also involves
> a careful division of labor between men and women: "Women tend
> gardens, pigs and children. They usually cook for the household and
> keep the house clean. Nowadays they do the washing, most market
> selling, a lot of coffee picking, and cleaning. Men prepare garden sites
> from bush (very infrequently; subsequent grass burnings of a plot is
> normally the work of women), hunt, transact exchanges, arrange pig
> kills, fight wars and lead religions." (Josephides 1985: 116)

Although it is not clear that most Kewa women at the time of Josephides's fieldwork would have described it as such, this is clearly a gendered system of exploitation, in which women's duties substantially outweigh men's. The key aspect of this division involves the fact that wives are responsible for raising pigs, which are the key form of wealth in local society. Wives also raise much of the food necessary to feed these pigs and their own family.

In spite of wives' importance in economic production, however, it is husbands who are responsible for trading pigs and for sacrificing and distributing them at ritual feasts. Women's labor in raising pigs is not generally recognized in any overt or public way, since social respect accrues to men during pig exchange and slaughter. While Josephides does not document a clear disparity in the standard of living of men and women, the place of women in society means that they are inevitably responsible for the most difficult, menial, and private tasks, while men are responsible for the most enjoyable, respected, and public tasks.

Among Josephides's Kewa informants, both men and women are constantly pressed into their separate tasks by the economic exigencies of daily life. Neither men nor women generally support the idea that women could take over men's roles in coordinating economic activity and organizing ritual feasts. Women might object to the basic inequality they are subjected to, but married adult women ultimately face overwhelming pressure from both the specific men who are their husbands and from society at large to conform to the economic duties laid out for them. In a turn of events that many of the readers of this book will recognize, women's role as caregivers is generally highlighted in this process. Cooperation in economic affairs between husbands and wives is consistently described as "helping the husband" and "lifting his worry" (Josephides 1985: 119).

The overall lesson to be had here is that the production of inequality is—or at least can be—a process that occurs across numerous domains of everyday life. Economic processes, political norms, gender identities, and ideological truths are merged together in everyday life. Inequality emerges from the combined character of these domains and is thus deeply woven into the fabric of everyday life. Accordingly, there is not generally a single causal account of inequality—we expect it to emerge from numerous aspects of cultural context. We could not say, for example, that the economic activities of Kewa women or the ideologies of Kewa gender identity are the primary source of Kewa gender inequality. Similarly, in this book I will frequently be addressing "forms of inequality"—such as political inequality, economic inequality, gender inequality, racial inequality, and so on. However, the distinction between these "forms" should not be taken as evidence that any one of them exists independently.

Plan of the Book

In the course of this short introduction, we have moved from some basic philosophical insights about anthropology and global inequality to real historical contexts and specific ethnographic cases. The plan of this book takes us in the opposite direction, from the daunting challenges posed by economic inequality on a global scale, through a series of questions about inequality within nation-states, and finally to a set of more insistently local concerns. In the closing paragraphs of this introduction, I offer a brief synopsis of each chapter.

Chapter 2 provides an historical overview of globalization. This chapter is intended largely as background. However, I return throughout to the theme of inequality, as well as to the contributions that anthropologists have made toward the understanding of inequality within the global economic system.

14   Chapter 3 attempts a basic interpretation of economic inequality as it exists on a global scale. Throughout this chapter, I ask how a large-scale view of economic globalization can be meaningful for individual ethnographers. I am specifically concerned here with a set of institutions (including the International Monetary Fund and the World Trade Organization), which will be familiar to many informed readers, as well as with a series of more academic debates about the sources of inequality between countries.

Chapter 4 shifts to more theoretical ground, focusing on the overlapping and self-reinforcing character of various forms of inequality. I begin with an analysis of gender inequality as it exists on a global scale, pointing out the ways in which local gender hierarchies can become fused into more clearly global forms. From there, I move on to a discussion of various ways in which different forms of inequality can help to reinforce one another.

Chapter 5 is the first of two chapters that discuss inequality specifically within the confines of the nation-state. In this first instance, I am concerned with political forms of inequality. When most people talk about fighting for equality, what they are concerned with are those forms of political and legal inequality that exist within the framework of nation-states. However, there are some obvious limits on equality of this type, and this chapter is largely dedicated to exploring those limits.

Chapter 6 continues to be concerned with the nation-state, turning to those issues of economic equality associated with the welfare state. In the contemporary world, the welfare state stands out as a powerful institution dedicated to the improvement of economic equality. Again, however, my concern is with the frequently severe limitations that exist for the welfare state as a national institution.

Chapter 7 is the first of two chapters wherein I consider various aspects of inequality more specifically from the point of view of everyday life. In this case, I am concerned with the possibilities for directly addressing inequality within local contexts through organized action.

Chapter 8 looks at some of the more subtle ways in which inequality seeps into everyday life. I am particularly concerned with describing how inequality is addressed through the very formation of cultural categories rather than through the overt action of those affected by inequality.

CHAPTER 2

GLOBAL INEQUALITY: HISTORICAL-ANTHROPOLOGICAL PERSPECTIVES

The historical starting point of the process of globalization cannot be clearly fixed. The mainstream view, however, is reflected in the contention of the anthropologist Michel-Rolph Trouillot (2003: 29) that "the world became global in the 16th century." Trouillot is referring specifically to the beginning of regular travel between the eastern and western hemispheres, as well as the first exertions of European colonial power around the world. By contrast, a minority of scholars have argued that globalization truly began only with the integration of national economies in the nineteenth century, and others still that the basic dynamic of globalization stretches back to the rise of ancient Egyptian and Mesopotamian civilizations.

Colonialism and Inequality in a Mercantile Age

If we follow the mainstream and date globalization to the sixteenth century, our attention is drawn very quickly to the economic system known as *merchant capitalism*. Under this system, wealthy merchants and government officials sought power through the direct control of trade between nations. To garner the "trading profits" (Braudel 1979: 168) crucial to the maintenance of this system, it was necessary to master complex global logistics and skillfully anticipate the fluctuations of prices in numerous far-off places. Governments sometimes attempted to exercise a direct monopoly over trade goods (such as the Portuguese attempt to monopolize the global pepper trade in the sixteenth century), but more often allowed private and semi-private corporations (such as the famous Dutch East India Company) to seek their own profits and, very often, to directly administer the nation's colonial holdings. Even when the colonial venture rested in private hands, however, the state depended on the taxation of trading profits to finance its activities. Stable domestic governance and strong militaries (including a global naval presence) were crucial for the success of the colonial endeavor.

There are good examples of concentrated forms of mercantile power beginning in the Islamic world more than 1,000 years ago. However, it was European expansion after 1500 that would allow merchant capitalists to form a web of trade with unprecedented scope. In this sense, the relationship between national colonial projects and merchant capital is quite clear: control of international trade became most desirable at the moment when there were new colonies to exploit and new colonial rivals to vanquish.

The eighteenth century was the high point of merchant capitalism. At this time, one could find great merchant houses in London (cf. Brewer 1990: ch. 6) whose power resembled that which had first been acquired by Islamic merchants in Mecca (cf. Ibrahim 1990: ch. 6) 1,000 years before. What had changed, however, was the scope of the mercantile project. Within the web of trade fueled by European colonialism, genuinely global forms of inequality began to emerge. The global slave trade—including various forms of indentured servitude and "coolie labor," as well as the 12 million native Africans enslaved and sold across the Atlantic—created a massive flow of people on the basis of a rather obvious power imbalance. The first global workforce consisted of people working under pain of death, thousands of miles from their homes. While merchant capitalism provided the coordination for this global trade in human beings, the global forms of inequality that emerged from this trade have important ramifications through to the present day.

The exploitation, displacement, and mass murder of indigenous people can similarly be interpreted as a form of global inequality with ongoing effects. If we consider their histories only up to contact with colonizing Europeans, many indigenous people in far-flung parts of the world might have little in common. However, it is by virtue of this contact and the colonial process that unfolded in its wake that many of these people can be said to share a 500-year history. In some parts of the world, such as the Caribbean, native populations were all but wiped out (through accidentally transmitted diseases and intentionally inflicted violence) and replaced by slave labor. In other parts of the world, such as the United States and Canada, large settler communities of European descent would displace the indigenous people who survived initial contact, famously forcing them further and further away from the colonial frontier in a form of colonization known as *settler colonialism*.

In still other parts of the world, existing native populations would provide the backbone of the local economy, providing the labor for the extraction of agricultural and mineral resources. In some cases, this *conquest colonialism* hinged on the ability of European producers to pay extremely low wages to local populations possessed of less developed technology. In many cases, however, colonized people were compelled to labor sporadically in mines or on plantations. Forced labor of indigenous populations was the norm in African colonialism, with places such as the Belgian Congo offering particularly brutal examples. Generally, such practices constituted a form of *corvée labor*, which involves only periodic forced labor. This contrasts with the *chattel slavery* well known by many students of US history. In many cases, taxes on native populations helped to compel participation in colonial labor schemes, particularly when those taxes were required to be paid directly in labor. Throughout this process, racial discrimination and economic motives were constantly intermingled. As the historian Walter Rodney (1974) has argued, colonial exploration occurred not only by virtue of profit motives, but also by virtue of outright racism. He gives the example of copper mines in the British colony of Northern Rhodesia (present-day Zimbabwe), where Europeans could receive wages 10 times higher than Africans who performed the same job.

Inequality and the World System of Industrial Capitalism

Historians continue to dispute the relationship between colonialism and the transition from merchant capitalism to industrial capitalism. Many argue that the possession of colonies cannot be described as an immediate cause of the Industrial Revolution in Europe (see, for discussion, Griffin 2010). It seems clear, however, that the new forms of industrial production that spread throughout Europe during the nineteenth century depended on raw materials harvested by the hands of slaves or other economically exploited colonial subjects. Concentrated at first in Europe, and spreading in small part to North America, the factories of the nineteenth century created vast wealth, allowing the growth of a new elite of capitalist entrepreneurs and a new urban proletariat of factory workers. Colonialism was a necessary, if not entirely sufficient, cause of this process.

The emergence of industrial capitalism as a transnational system did not run a straight course. Roughly concurrent with the peak of the Industrial Revolution, the era of colonialist globalization reached its height in 1860, with the signing of a free trade agreement between France and the United Kingdom. Forged between the two greatest colonial powers (which comprised, of course, the world's two largest economies), this agreement ushered in a new age of open economic cooperation between powerful Western European countries. Since at least the second half of the nineteenth century, the lowering of tariffs (i.e., taxes on imports), has been crucial to global economic growth.

Protectionism, or the reimposition of previously reduced tariffs, would reemerge in Europe as a response to periodic economic shocks (such as the global depression that followed the financial crisis of 1873). However, it was the "Great War" itself that occasioned the greatest reversals of global integration, leaving individual countries more isolated and global trade networks vastly diminished. It was only after World War II that trade relationships would recover to the level they reached before World War I.

The current mechanisms for the inegalitarian distribution of wealth across countries hinges on a pattern of open but unequal exchange that became prevalent at the end of the colonial era. Social theorists such as Immanuel Wallerstein (who styles himself a "world system analyst") have argued that rich countries in the contemporary global economy have been able to consistently control the most profitable forms of economic production through a series of short-term *quasi-monopolies* (Wallerstein 2004: 28). These quasi-monopolies involve short-term advantages in technological sophistication, legal protection, and the like. In some cases, a quasi-monopoly might be protected by the fact that imitators simply haven't succeeded yet. In other cases, patent laws may play a crucial role in ensuring that the profits from a certain type of production are steered to particular firms.

Using Wallerstein's terminology, the sorts of economic advantage provided by quasi-monopolies can be said to divide the world into "core" (i.e., rich) countries, "semi-peripheral" (i.e., poor) countries, and "peripheral" (i.e., extremely poor) countries. The very fact that the world is divided into rich and poor countries is usually taken for granted, but what social scientists such as Wallerstein have argued is that this division is not naturally occurring. In spite of the entire discourse of "development" (which has been amply deconstructed by the anthropologist James Ferguson [1990]), the divisions between rich and poor countries are due more to entrenched advantages and institutional manipulation than they are to hard work or innovation. To borrow from the political economist Samir Amin (1976: 148–49), the global division of rich and poor countries engendered through industrial capitalism after World War II has been the more simple result of the sort of "unequal exchanges" that occur "whenever labor of the same productivity is rewarded at a lower rate in the periphery" than it is in the core of the global economy.

The inequity to which Amin points is not the fault of any one person or group. Similarly, the self-reinforcing character of the advantages borne by the residents of rich countries cannot simply be wished away. Profits achieved at one moment in time encourage the development of new technologies (and new industries based on these technologies), which in turn allows rich countries to monopolize higher profits going forward. When poor countries "inherit" the old technologies no longer on the cutting edge, they do so on a basis that allows for little accumulation of capital. While these technologies remain useful, they serve much less successfully as the basis for creating wealth. Ultimately, the residents of poor countries have few opportunities to move toward the "technological frontier" where profits are dependable and robust.

Altogether, this dynamic has come to be identified with the notion of *underdevelopment* (see Frank 1966 for the first use of this term). Poor countries are almost always behind in their ability to implement technological innovations. In a world where capital investment is directed toward the frontier established by new technologies, this inevitably means a vicious circle of poverty and low economic growth. It is much easier for poor countries to serve as a source of raw materials and as a market for a small amount of excess industrial goods than it is for them to leap forward and become their own hubs of capital investment and industrial production. Noting this arrangement, some skeptics (see Hirst, Thompson, and Bromley 2009) have questioned whether anything like globalization in fact exists, since there is no genuinely open flow of capital investment across borders. To me, this sort of broad skepticism about the very concept of globalization is unwarranted; it is more precise to say that economic globalization does indeed exist, in spite of the fact that it is partially checked by national and cultural boundaries.

Of course, it is also important to note that globalization is not an entirely economic process and has been deeply influenced by the actions of nation-states. Most crucially, the governments of rich countries managed to confine high-profit industries to their native shores by strategically imposing tariffs to protect developing industries and only promoting free trade once "industrial supremacy" had been achieved in a particular area (Chang 2002: 5). This approach had the effect of allowing domestic industries to develop, while still contributing to global economic growth. To borrow a phrase from the economist Ha-Joon Chang (2002), rich countries have remained at the edge of technological and economic development by "kicking away the ladder" of protectionist policies that they themselves climbed up. For most of the twentieth century, this dynamic resulted in the concentration of industrial production in Europe, North America, and Japan. Attempts to industrialize elsewhere were sporadic at best and largely resulted in failure.

An important exception to this was the "second world" of socialist countries dominated by the Soviet Union. With authoritarian control over civil society and politics, carefully controlled economic barriers with the outside world, and a carefully planned industrialization strategy, the state socialist countries of the East Bloc managed to slowly close the gap with the rich countries of the "first world" until economic stagnation set in during the 1970s. After the fall of the Berlin Wall and the end of state socialism, industrial production fell dramatically across Eastern Europe and Russia, tragically reversing many of the economic advantages that were achieved at great cost under authoritarian regimes.

19

The 1980s and 1990s were marked not only by the collapse of state socialism, but also by the rise of the "Asian Tigers"—a set of countries in East Asia where increasingly technical forms of industrial production successfully took root. Buoyed by new industries in South Korea and Taiwan, these countries gradually moved toward the forward edge of high-technology industrial production. More recently, massive industrialization in China (see Chapter 8) has also been an important factor in the global division of wealth. While many people in China remain extremely poor, industrialization has allowed some—at the cost of backbreaking labor—to move toward the global middle class. Since the 1990s, globalization has entered a new phase, with some arguing that "the 21st century will be Asian" or "the next phase of globalization will most likely have an Asian face" (Frank 2004). Based in particular on the ongoing process of economic change in Asia, it no longer seems that the heights of the industrial economy will be confined to the same countries that led globalization throughout the twentieth century.

Some have speculated that changes in globalization will mean a fall by the United States from its role as global economic and military leader in favor of China. In the medium term, it certainly seems at least possible that economic growth in China will help usher in a new "multi-polar" world of major powers also including the United States and the European Union (Pieterse 2009: xiii–xxvii). It is also possible that economic growth in China will falter, as it did in the Soviet socialist system half a century ago. Beyond these concerns about the future, however, lies the more important question of whether other countries can even begin to replicate China's path toward industrial development. Large, moderate-income countries such as Brazil, India, and Indonesia are obvious candidates for this sort of transformation. As Chang has pointed out, there is also the hope that reasonable development policies and fair transnational arrangements would also help even the poorest countries of the world—overwhelmingly concentrated in Africa—to commence in sustainable economic development (see Pieterse 2009: xiii–xxvii).

Anthropology in a Postcolonial World

Most colonies in Africa, Asia, and the Caribbean were liberated between the end of World War II and the early 1970s, as European powers retreated and a series of "new states" were created. These decolonized countries would join their former colonizers in a new "community of nations" symbolized by the institution of the United Nations. However, they would also remain in a distinctly postcolonial space, both in the sense that the crimes of colonialism remained unredeemed and in the sense that ongoing inequalities are, up to this day, rooted in colonial divisions.

As historical-anthropological research by anthropologists such as Jason Hickel (2012) has tended to show, people living in postcolonial countries could not simply count on a return to tradition to establish political institutions. The tactic of indirect rule, whereby colonial authorities erected ostensibly traditional institutions to maintain order, made any claims regarding "tradition" into particularly suspect ones. The problematic relationship with the past in the postcolonial world has been mirrored by a reassessment within anthropology of what it means to speak of a particular culture as having its own unique customs and traditions. As I argued in the previous chapter, the long-standing tendency within anthropology to conceive of individual, isolated cultures should not be taken as an indication that these sorts of cultures actually exist. In recent years, anthropologists have drawn attention to the ways in which a category such as "custom" can "become a trope for a society which was outside of history and devoid of individuals" (Dirks 1997: 210).

The postcolonial context has been a crucial one for anthropologists to think out the complexities that exist beyond these sorts of notions, in an interconnected and interdependent world where "native cultures" cannot be discretely contained or neatly separated from the results of colonial contact. Anthropologists have drawn attention to the ways in which colonizing cultures were themselves divided, as well as the ways in which the experience of colonization deeply shaped these same colonizing cultures (see Comaroff 1989; Stoler 1995). Moreover, projects such as these have supported the conclusion of the postcolonial theorist Homi Bhabha (1994: 63) that the "image" of a colonized other is "deeply woven into the psychic pattern of the West." The sorts of political freedom and agency that have been valorized in European political discourse since at least the eighteenth century are hard to imagine without some specifically colonial encounter.

Trouillot, quoted at the beginning of this chapter, has urged colleagues to address "the politics and poetics of otherness," arguing that the "Savage slot" effectively established by early anthropological writings remains, as essentialized others continue to be incorporated into anthropological narratives even in the postcolonial age. Writing in 1991 (and republished in 2003: 9), Trouillot argued that "anthropology's future depends largely on its ability to contest the Savage slot and the *thématique* that constructs this slot." To date, however, it remains unclear whether Trouillot's goals have been successfully achieved. Anthropologists still find other people to study, and the question of whether or not they do so to shore up their own identity as more ordered, more civilized, and more knowing persons remains an open one.

Anthropologists Confront the World System (and Each Other)

In his *Europe and the People Without History*, the anthropologist Eric Wolf provided one of the earliest and most forceful justifications for anthropological concern with the world system as described by Immanuel Wallerstein.

Wolf (1997: 3) begins his case in this way: "The world of humankind constitutes a manifold, a totality of interconnected processes.... Inquiries that disassemble this totality into bits and then fail to reassemble it falsify reality. Concepts like 'nation,' 'society,' and 'culture' name bits and threaten to turn names into things. Only by understanding these names as bundles of relationships, and by placing them back into the field from which they were abstracted, can we hope to avoid misleading inferences and increase our share of understanding."

He further argues that "we shall not understand the present world unless we trace the growth of the world market and the course of capitalist development" (21).

From this argument flow a host of details regarding the earliest global links between economic livelihoods. Wolf tells us, for example, that "by 1670 sites of the Onondaga subgroup of the Iroquois reveal almost no items of native manufacture" (1997: 4), thereby indicating the rapidity with which European settlers and indigenous Americans were incorporated into a single trade economy. He further tells us about how Islam spread to South Asia 1,000 years ago, how peasant populations emerged in northern Colombia after 1870, and how African states under French colonial control played a key role in cocoa cultivation on the Ivory Coast several decades later. Throughout these sorts of cases, we see native and *metropolitan* (the term used for people who live in the *metropole*, or center of colonial domination) cultures coming together through contact, interaction, and, above all, the movement of workers and economic goods.

Closely associated with Wolf's book is another by the anthropologist Sidney Mintz (1985). Entitled *Sweetness and Power: The Place of Sugar in Modern History*, this book seeks to draw global connections by tracing the history of sugar production and consumption. Mintz shows how sugar planters, at first in the Mediterranean and later in the Caribbean and South America, drew on slave labor to create a mammoth industry. However, the rise of sugar required new consumers as well, and the introduction of sugar into daily life in Europe quickly became crucial for the mercantile economy. Mintz traces the consumption of sugar in its most mundane forms (e.g., as an additive to tea) as well as in its most extravagant ones (e.g., the modern form of wedding cakes initiated in 1830s England). The result is an image of a world brought together by a single commodity, but sharply divided between producers and consumers.

While both of these books succeeded in introducing a global perspective to the discipline of anthropology, it was noticeable that neither of them involved ethnographic research. Wolf had completed fieldwork in Mexico and Italy early in his career, but moved later to focus on historical work on the broad scale evoked in *Europe and the People Without History*. Mintz had an even longer track record of ethnographic fieldwork in the

Caribbean, but *Sweetness and Power* notably does not include even a shred of ethnographic evidence to help make its case. Indeed, Mintz's book is notably a history of sugar's production and consumption narrated from a highly removed perspective. It is only on the 174th page that he comes to the "point that the ideas of meaning and power touch" his analysis, and even this seems largely an aside to his historical project.

This lack of ethnographic engagement was not lost on critics. The anthropologist Michael Taussig (1989: 13) rounded on Mintz as being "so terribly staid, so framed, cognitive, and uptight." For Taussig, a history of sugar dictated from an abstract and "Archimedean" perspective could only be a failure—a failure to meaningfully engage with the lives of the people actually affected by the sugar trade, a failure to understand the nature of money and exchange in the modern world, a failure to grasp what was at stake in colonialism, and, above all, a failure to understand how the trade in commodities can replace more meaningful relationships between people. Taussig, whose critique of Mintz centers on the notions of *reification* and *fetishization*, points to the way that slave labor all but disappears in the creation of a commodity that is so apparently sweet. Consuming sugar in Europe, one did not easily detect the bitterness of the slave's experience— just as one can hardly detect the brutal conditions of a Bangladeshi or Indonesian textile factory every time one dons a white t-shirt today.

Taussig's own research has centered on the way that people in Colombia have encountered capitalism. In his first book, *The Devil and Commodity Fetishism in South America*, he built on his own fieldwork and that of the anthropologist June Nash in nearby Bolivia to argue that the introduction of capitalist relations of production to the area involved "radically different concepts of creation, life, and growth" (Taussig 1980: 17). Local peasants who were displaced from their lands and became incorporated into plantation agriculture (Colombia) and tin mining (Bolivia) frequently interpreted capitalist relations of production to involve some sort of nefarious and supernatural force. These landless laborers were in a situation in which, no matter how hard they worked, it remained all but impossible to alter their basic social position as indigent laborers. The result, according to Taussig, is a worldview that molds the facts of existence under capitalism to surprisingly novel ends.

Most famously, Taussig detailed a case in which plantation workers describe the use of small figurines known as *muñecos* (dolls) to speed up their work and derive extra wages. According to beliefs shared by these workers, the use of these figurines required a contract with the devil. However, the same workers also believed that the use of a *muñeco* would result in wages that were cursed, such that they could not be used as an investment in a new enterprise but could be spent only on relative luxuries and frittered away on "fine clothes, liquor, butter, and so on" (Taussig 1980: 94–95).

The result is a view of the world in which hard work is understood to be cursed, rather than a source of economic value. Similar to a set of cases discussed in Chapter 6, the realization of wealth under capitalism is linked to infernal and supernatural powers.

What Taussig argues is that this interpretation of capitalism is, in its own way, quite sensible. How else to explain an economic system in which wealth reproduces itself, and any attempt to escape a dispossessed status all but inevitably fails? The landless laborers and miners described by Taussig are stuck in an economic role that generates profits for other people, but only allows the most meager existence for workers. The distinction between wages and profits, as well as the distinction between ordinary forms of work and cursed forms of overwork, might quite reasonably acquire a cosmic significance under these circumstances.

Between Global History and Local Ethnography

Taussig's critique of Mintz and Wolf (who also responded to Taussig in print—see Mintz and Wolf 1989) is emblematic of the ongoing conflict within anthropology between global histories and local ethnographies. A good way to examine this conflict further is through the work of June Nash, the anthropologist whom Taussig borrowed from extensively in the book described above. Like Taussig, Nash is deeply concerned with the effects of capitalist economies in local contexts. Her fieldwork includes miners in Bolivia and peasants in the Chiapas region of southern Mexico, both groups situated rather clearly on the periphery of Wallerstein's world system. However, she also carried out fieldwork in the US town of Pittsfield, Massachusetts, where General Electric manufactured weapons for many decades and exercised a certain "corporate hegemony" over the local community.

Some parts of Nash's scholarship might be seen as a bridge between the sort of global history envisioned by Wolf and Mintz on the one hand, and the insistently local and experiential ethnography practiced by Taussig on the other. Nash's 2001 monograph *Mayan Visions: The Quest for Autonomy in an Age of Globalization* is particularly notable in this regard. Her fieldwork in the Chiapas region of southern Mexico stretches back to the 1950s, when Mayan villages were mostly insulated from the outside world. Although the Mexican revolution had implemented important land reforms, these often favored local *ladino* populations—that is, the Spanish-speaking people of Hispanic or mixed indigenous-Hispanic ancestry. Indigenous people were disadvantaged both in the political hierarchy centered on far-off Mexico City, and in the local agricultural economy.

Neoliberal economic policies implemented beginning in the 1980s (see the next chapter) caused a substantial decrease in food prices, further disadvantaging local indigenous farmers in Chiapas. The result of these processes included the growth of low-income barrios surrounding the regional center of San Cristóbal de las Casas and the encroachment of indigenous farmers on nearby jungle wilderness preserves. Notably, however, there was also a strong militant reaction against the Mexican government, which was widely seen as indifferent to the plight of local indigenous people. The EZLN (an organization whose full name translates as Zapatista Army of National Liberation) began an offensive against local government representatives. This offensive was timed to begin immediately following the commencement of a new free trade treaty with the United States, which was widely understood to be detrimental to the interests of local indigenous farmers. The Zapatistas (as the EZLN was known) were primarily concerned with the autonomy of the indigenous Mayan community from the Mexican government, especially within the several dozen villages which had been intermittently under the Zapatistas' own control.

Nash's ethnography of the Mayan community in Chiapas focuses on this drive for autonomy. She traces the militant activities of the Zapatista movement and the various attempts by the government to either suppress or bargain with its members. Along the way, she argues several key points: first, that local communities share a single *habitus*, or habitual patterns of social action; second, that the Mayan community in Chiapas went through a radical change around the time of the Zapatista uprising, reorienting local actors to various forms of national and transnational politics; and third, that these same people saw themselves primarily as an ethnic group deserving a specifically ethnic form of autonomy. During the 1990s, the Zapatistas networked with political allies in Mexico (including other indigenous groups) and with leftist intellectuals in Europe (including the well-known sociologist Alain Touraine, whose descriptions of the Zapatista cause from the perspective of an activist and scholar were sometimes controversial).

Nash (2001: 235, 213) describes the Zapatista movement (and other related Mayan social movements) as attempts to develop "heterodox" ethnic identities within a "pluricultural" nation. According to this account, ethnic identity can be both open and inclusive, and involves a shared striving for social justice as much as some shared interpretation of essential ethnic characteristics. It is controversial, to say the least, whether this sort of model of an open and oppositional ethnic indigenous identity can provide a feasible basis for political action and fair economic relationships in a place like Chiapas, much less elsewhere in the world. What does seem clear, however, is that Nash (219) regards the attempt to build this kind of heterodox ethnic community as a corrective to those global economic forces that have tended to impoverish indigenous people. Her vision, to borrow from one of her chapter titles, is of indigenous people and their "pluricultural survival in the global ecumene."

Conclusion

Somewhat more recently than Nash, the anthropologist Anna Lowenhaupt Tsing (2005) has attempted to create an ethnography of how global forces play out in her fieldsite in a remote part of Indonesia. Tsing is less convinced than Nash of the possibilities for local ethnic identities as a source of political struggle. She describes the way in which a global market for forest products affects everyday life in Indonesia, as indigenous people face the loss of their homes and livelihoods through deforestation, and learn to organize and fight back alongside environmental activists. However, Tsing argues that the local indigenous community is not the only group affected by globalization. She also sees global forces at work in the way that college students from the city of Yogyakarta romanticize the forest as a place apart from Indonesian national politics. The result is a complicated set of relationships between international trade, indigenous people, and national activists.

Ultimately, Tsing comes to the surprisingly plainspoken conclusions that "to 'think globally' is no easy task" because "global capitalism" is inherently "messy" (2005: 2, 11). She describes that the only way she can think to describe the relationship between her local fieldsite and global economic forces is "patchwork and haphazard" (xi). While I am sympathetic with Tsing's predicament as an ethnographer seeking to link the global and the local, I disagree with the notion that even her own work is haphazard. When Tsing describes the way that the global market for timber products affects her fieldsite, and how deforestation reverberates across various parts of Indonesian society, this is not merely a haphazard account of disjointed lives. Rather, it suggests that there are new kinds of connections that have to be considered in light of the global economic forces. Most prominent among these are the relationships between indigenous people and nongovernmental activists. Tsing's account of these relationships does not line up neatly with Nash's vision of a "heterodox" ethnic community within a "pluricultural" nation. But this is precisely the point—in each ethnography, global connections must be described in a novel manner. While the result might be a variety of ethnographic descriptions that do not neatly line up, the past gives us at least some hope that anthropologists' long engagement with globalization—and with each other—will continue to refine our understanding.

CHAPTER 3

THE CHALLENGE OF GLOBAL INEQUALITY

Global Inequality—A Challenge to Anthropology

We live in a world of extreme inequality. No statistical measure of inequality is perfect, but most economists at least begin with one known as the Gini coefficient. This coefficient ranges from 0 to 1, with 0 representing perfect equality (everyone in the group has the same amount of income or wealth) and 1 representing perfect inequality (one person in the group has all the income or wealth). When this measure is applied to income, the most egalitarian country in the world is Denmark, with a Gini coefficient of .24, and the most inegalitarian country of any size is Namibia, with a Gini coefficient of .64. However, the world as a whole is estimated to have a Gini coefficient of between .61 and .71 (United Nations Development Programme 2010: 73). That is to say, the world as a whole is approximately as unequal as the most unequal country in the world.

The reason for this is simple: the poorest people in the world are heavily concentrated in low-income and middle-income countries.[1] Two-fifths of the global population lives on less than $2 a day, and virtually none of these people are in rich countries such as the United States and Canada. Instead, they live in poor countries (such as Namibia and Haiti) or moderate-income countries (such as Brazil and South Africa). Even more surprising than this lopsided distribution of poverty is the overall global distribution of income. Global inequality today means that there is a very small class of those who

---

1   The development economist Andy Sumner (2010) has recently pointed out that many of the world's poorest people actually live in middle-income countries.

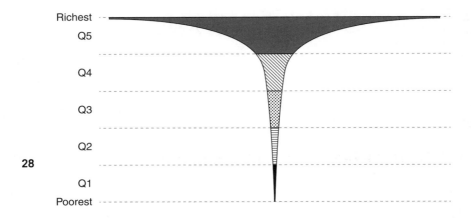

Figure 3.1 Global distribution of income. The broader bands toward the top represent higher incomes. Q1–Q5 represent quintiles of the global population.
Source: Adapted from Ortiz and Cummins 2011.

are extremely wealthy, followed by a moderately sized middle class whose incomes cover a broad span (many of them would be considered poor if they lived in a rich country). Below this middle class, however, are a very large number of people who live in varying degrees of extreme poverty. The chart in Figure 3.1 presents these facts visually.

The two things that are most striking about this chart are, first, the extremely high incomes represented for those at the top of the scale and, second, the extremely large number of people at the bottom sharing a very small percentage of the world's overall income. Roughly one-fifth of the global population lives on less than $1.25 a day, and another fifth lives on something between $1.25 and $2 a day. If all the income in the world were divided evenly, each person in the world would live on about $28 a day (or $10,220 per year). However, only people in the top fifth of the global population actually earn that much. The person at the middle of the global income distribution—also called the *median* person—actually receives something more like $8 a day, or $2,920 per year (Phelps and Crabtree 2013).

For ethnographers, statistics are meaningful only insofar as they illuminate relationships among the people we study. What are we therefore to make of the above facts from an anthropological perspective? In Chapter 1, I argued that inequality matters because relationships matter. But what can we know about those unequal relationships that exist on a global level? For example, to say that I have a relationship with the Chinese factory workers who built my cell phone might be to stretch our ordinary use of the word *relationship*. At best, I might be able to pinpoint the factory where this phone was made. Even then, this information would mean very little.

The average resident of a rich country and the much poorer people who do factory work in a country such as China have little clear insight into one another's lives.

The anthropologists Edward F. Fischer and Peter Blair Benson (2006: 172) have referred to these sorts of relationships as "connections between unknowing consumers and producers." In their own ethnography, Fischer and Benson attempt to describe the relationship between the desires of poor Mayan farmers who grow broccoli and the desires of health-conscious consumers in rich countries who consume that crop. Without a doubt, this research is full of startling juxtapositions. However, there is little that Fischer and Benson can do to actually bring together the lives of their two groups of distinct informants. This kind of project might be inherently interesting for the contrasts it creates, but it hardly helps us to constitute an anthropological analysis of global inequality.

A different sort of project that has begun to emerge in recent years focuses our ethnographic gaze directly on those elites who are most responsible for coordinating global relationships. A good example of such research is that recently performed by Douglas R. Holmes. National currencies (including the euro, which is a kind of supranational currency) are managed by central banks, whose leaders have a great deal of influence on the overall course of economic production in many countries. Holmes's ethnography (2009) encompasses central bankers in the United States, the United Kingdom, and Germany (at both the European and the German central banks). Similar research involving the Central Bank of Japan has been carried out by Annelise Riles (2004). As Holmes is quick to point out, however, these sorts of projects are as likely to turn into a collaboration between highly powerful actors and the ethnographers studying them as they are to remain a disinterested ethnography (see Holmes and Marcus 2008). While collaboration is almost universally valued as a positive aspect of ethnography, this particular sort of collaboration raises questions about the ability of ethnographers to use elite institutions as a vantage from which to understand unequal global relationships, rather than simply to have their work be appropriated by powerful political and economic actors. Overall, it seems quite clear that anthropologists cannot—at least not easily—study global inequality by performing an ethnography of the most powerful people responsible for managing that inequality.

When I was in graduate school, the instructors in my main course on anthropological theory would finish every class session by asking, "So what is the research agenda that we can get from all of this?" If we have established global inequality as an important object of inquiry, we would be well advised to at least pose this question. Clearly, I believe that the entire solution rests neither with parallel ethnographies of rich and poor people nor with ethnographies of global institutional elites. I do, however, have some modest suggestions. While these may not constitute a full-blown research agenda, I think that they do tend in that direction.

- First, anthropologists should be generally aware of the sorts of institutional arrangements that mediate inequality on a global level. Knowledge about these institutions can come from many different sources—it might include statistics or economic analysis, it might include accounts of relevant events in the media or elsewhere in the academic literature, and it might also include ethnographic research on the leaders of these institutions such as that undertaken by Holmes and Riles. In the first section below, I attempt to give an example of this sort of *context-building*.
- Second, these institutional arrangements can be subject to an anthropological analysis that is itself not necessarily ethnographic. That is to say, there are times when it is appropriate for anthropologists to address topics of global importance in a way that advances anthropological knowledge without necessarily engaging a particular ethnographic context. Insofar as anthropologists are able to establish some base of knowledge about global inequality, they should be able to subject this knowledge to anthropological theory directly, without necessarily filtering it through the lens of ethnography. Applying David Graeber's ideas about debt to transnational institutions such as the International Money Fund (IMF), I attempt this sort of *theory-building* exercise in the second section below.
- Third, and finally, it seems to me that anthropologists should be able to respond to the sorts of context-building and theory-building work that occurs in other social scientific disciplines. In the third section below, I attempt to answer two economic historians who have attempted to make arguments about culture as a source of modern economic inequality. This exercise of *contestation* is intended specifically to have implications beyond the disciplinary boundaries of anthropology.

Globalization as Free Trade and "Harmonization"

Beginning in 1947, the World Trade Organization (WTO, previously known as the General Agreement on Tariffs and Trade) was responsible for a series of multilateral agreements between nations, according to which tariffs and other barriers to trade were reduced by all parties. Since the mid-1990s, however, regional trade agreements enacted on a smaller scale have gained in relevance, pushing much of the WTO's unilateralist approach to trade agreements to the side. These regional agreements include the North

American Free Trade Agreement (NAFTA), the Southern Common Market (Mercosur), and the ASEAN Free Trade Area (AFTA).

Trade agreements are signed by national governments as well as by the European Union on behalf of its member nations. The growth in regional trade agreements has led to what US trade officials have called "competitive liberalization"—that is, attempts by different groups of countries to open trade with one another in such a way that gives them an advantage over countries outside such agreements. In this sense, different trade agreements can be seen to compete with one another. For rich countries, this arrangement is highly congenial—their large economies mean that they carry larger amounts of leverage in negotiations with various groups of poorer countries. By the same token, trade agreements between poor countries have only minimal significance in the larger global economy, since by definition they do not create new types of access to the world's biggest markets. The result of this lopsided process has been a series of agreements, which have been described by one former WTO official and Wall Street banker as "a bullying opportunity" enacted on a global scale (Jones 2007: 5).

To understand the sorts of asymmetric relationships that exist between rich and poor countries involved in regional trade agreements, it is helpful to turn to a concrete example. To understand this example, it is first important to know that free trade agreements today have less and less to do with the reduction of tariffs and increasingly involve the "harmonization" of local regulations. Beginning in 2006, the government of Thailand granted a series of government-use patents for drugs used to treat HIV, vascular disease, and cancer. These patents allowed the Thai government to import generic versions of the drugs in question at a much lower cost than those offered by the pharmaceutical companies that first invented and marketed them. With the interests of US-based pharmaceutical companies in mind, the US government retaliated against this move by imposing new duties on three categories of Thai products regularly imported to the United States (Yamabhai et al. 2011).

Crucially, the US imposition of these duties has an effect not only on export-oriented industries, but also on public health in Thailand. National sovereignty is at stake in cases like these, in the sense that "trade agreements" frequently dictate what types of health, labor, consumer, and environmental policies a government is permitted to maintain. Governments in poor and middle-income countries have to choose between the competitive pressure to join regional trade agreements and the desire to maintain specific policy goals. In the case of Thailand, the die has been cast in favor of membership in trade agreements. In 2012, the government of Thailand expressed a wish to join the Trans-Pacific Partnership (TPP), a trade agreement currently being negotiated by the United States and 11 other countries on the Pacific Rim. Although negotiations are still underway at the time of this writing, the United States has exerted a great deal of pressure on these potential partners to outlaw government-use patents of the type described above. Such rules would "harmonize" patent law and public health policy, so that all countries in question would agree, for example, to import only more expensive, brand-name drugs rather than their generic equivalents.

The problems with this arrangement have been succinctly stated by the economist Joseph Stiglitz:

> Tariffs around the world are already low. The focus has shifted to "nontariff barriers," and the most important of these—for the corporate interests pushing agreements—are regulations. Huge multinational corporations complain that inconsistent regulations make business costly. But most of the regulations, even if they are imperfect, are there for a reason: to protect workers, consumers, the economy and the environment. (Stiglitz 2014: n.p.)

In the contemporary world, the "harmonization" of laws and policies via trade agreements amounts to a race to the bottom, ensuring that each country offers the lowest common denominator of protections to public health, to a free Internet, and to the rights of workers and consumers. As of this writing, some aspects of the secretly negotiated Transatlantic Trade and Investment Partnership (TTIP) between the United States and the European Union have leaked. These include provisions that would require an independent process screening the laws enacted by democratically elected legislators and a special arbitration panel that would allow foreign companies to sue for lost profits attributable to policies that have not been properly "harmonized."

From the point of view of an engaged global citizen, negotiations carried out secretly among government elites highly beholden to corporate interests are a problem. There is simply no good reason why global trade agreements cannot actually improve robust protections for consumers and workers, and for ordinary environmental and public health purposes. The main difficulty with achieving these goals is the lack of widespread public engagement in the formation of regional trade agreements. While a modestly sized protest movement across Europe has emerged in opposition to the TTIP, this is the rare exception. The fact that transnational trade agreements are deliberately negotiated in secret makes it extremely difficult to have serious debate about the specific provisions they contain.

For ethnographers, the problem is both that trade agreements such as these are negotiated in secret and that the effects of these trade agreements are generally too diffuse to study through participant observation. There are some opportunities to purposefully seek out fieldsites where competitive liberalization is meaningful as a fact on the ground, for example by studying the previously mentioned European protest movement against the TTIP. Beyond this, however, ethnographers wishing to address the relevant issues would be forced into a series of ancillary fieldsites. For example, it is possible to think about how national political discourses are constituted in such a way as to exclude discussions about transnational agreements. However, this requires that ethnographers manage to address the formation of political discourse (through the production and consumption of news media, for example) while also taking the extra step to consider what this process of formation specifically does *not* include. Without a doubt, this is a very roundabout means to address an important topic. However, such a **33** hypothetical project does pose an important object lesson in the necessity of considering the types of institutional context that can be quite invisible in the course of locally situated fieldwork.

The "Washington Consensus" and the Morality of Debt

Of course, it is not necessary that anthropologists confine themselves to such deeply contextual, highly roundabout means to study global inequality. In recent years, growing concern among anthropologists about neoliberal economic ideologies has opened a possibility for more directly addressing the transnational institutional arrangements that mediate unequal relationships operating on a global scale.

Neoliberal ideologies are sets of ideas linked to the so-called classical liberalism of eighteenth- and nineteenth-century political economists, such as Adam Smith and David Ricardo, who were early proponents of private enterprise and free trade. According to neoliberal ideology, markets can distribute goods most efficiently when there is a minimum of government intervention. Particularly since the 1980s, neoliberal ideas have been supported by the powerful governments of rich countries and the transnational institutions sometimes grouped together under the rubric of the "Washington Consensus." These institutions include the IMF, the World Bank, and the WTO. Among anthropologists, neoliberalism has generally had a "bad reputation" (Freeman 2007: 252), as it involves the imposition of strict free-market policies by national and transnational elites.

The institution that has been most clearly associated with the notion of neoliberalism is the IMF. In official terms, the main purpose of this institution is to provide the last line of defense against bankruptcy for insolvent debtor nations. Because it lends money to countries in crisis, the IMF has the power to extract substantial conditions from the governments to which it lends. These conditions are generally referred to as "Structural Adjustment Programs" and most frequently involve cutting government budgets (to free up money for interest payments) and raising interest rates on local currency (to encourage capital investments made in that local currency).

Critics of the IMF argue that cutting government budgets and raising interest rates at times of crisis can reinforce the downward momentum of the national economies affected by structural adjustment.[2] Defenders of the IMF respond that loans from that organization are always optional, and are designed only for countries willing to sacrifice short-term spending and low interest rates in favor of long-term growth. Crucially, IMF programs are good for the creditors of poor nations, since IMF loans help these nations to avoid defaulting on their debt.[3]

34   In 2011, the anthropologist David Graeber published a book entitled *Debt: The First 5,000 Years*, a second edition of which appeared in 2014. This book was remarkable for several reasons. To begin with, it was written for a popular audience and engaged a broad readership beyond academia. More important to the content of the book, however, was that it was organized as an encompassing history of the concept of debt, operating across numerous cultures and five millennia. Graeber's stated ambition with the book was to engage "Great Questions"—in this case, to explain the central role that debt has in shaping all manner of human relationships. Graeber's concerns include the notions that debt historically preceded money as a way of keeping track of economic obligations, that widespread coinage of money emerged as a response to the need to pay soldiers for warfare, and that the periodic blanket forgiveness of debts in the form of a "jubilee" has often been necessary to avoid the rampant growth of inequality. In accordance with a broad range of anthropologists, Graeber also comes to the very general conclusion that concerns about debt are frequently couched in moral terms (see Peebles 2010: 225).

Graeber is rather pointed about the fact that his most immediate concerns very much focus on the neoliberal policies of the IMF. He offers a "Biblical-style Jubilee affecting both consumer and international debt" as

---

2   For a classical example of this process, see the discussion of the Mexican case in Harvey (2005: 98–104). Also see discussion of the Haitian case in Loewenstein (2013: ch. 6).

3   Government debt crises frequently grow out of balance of payment crises, which occur when countries import more goods than they export. One country that has proven largely immune to balance of payment crises is the United States. Prior to the 2008 financial crisis, the United States regularly imported hundreds of billions of dollars of goods and services more than it exported. Since the crisis, this balance of payments has been cut in half, but it still continues to be by far the largest in the world. In either case, the reason why the United States can afford to import more than it exports is that international debt is largely denominated in dollars. A high debt balance by the inhabitants of United States weakens the dollar and therefore makes this debt easier to pay off. The French politician Valéry Giscard D'Estaing referred to this dynamic as involving the US's "exorbitant privilege" in global financial markets. Although the technical explanation of exorbitant privilege can be complicated, the key point is that because the dollar works as the global currency of choice, the inhabitants of the United States are generally able to consume more than they produce. For other countries, high balances of payment over the long term are instead an inevitable source of crisis. This is not likely to be the case for the United States until such time as some other currency becomes the most preferred means for the denomination of debt in the global financial market.

his single practical proposal against contemporary inequality and specifically cites the challenge to the IMF by "global justice movement" protestors as his impetus for writing the book. He recounts telling one interlocutor at a cocktail party that "thirty years of money flowing from the poorest countries to the richest was quite enough" (2014: 2).

For my purposes here, what is most interesting about Graeber's research is his attempt to redefine the debts of poor countries on an anthropological basis. A crucial aspect of neoliberal ideology involves the notion that markets are autonomously functioning and that debts can therefore be absolved only by economic means—that is, by their repayment. But Graeber insists, again and again, on something very different: that debts cannot be separated from their social context and that their repayment needs to take a broad set of social relations into account. This means, for example, that we have to consider whether or not the repayment of debt to institutional lenders will encourage global inequality.

On a broader basis, Graeber's thesis about the social character of debt also means that we have to think about debt in terms of a well-established anthropological theme, *the morality of exchange*. His insistence that, in historical terms, debt preceded money has an important corollary in the notion that debt is a social bond, one which can be used to draw people together into reciprocity and interdependence. The notion that it is possible to lend money to someone—or to an entire nation—and have nothing else to do with that person is deeply problematic. Graeber seeks to revive an old anthropological truism that acts of exchange do not simply leave people separated from one another, but rather contribute to the constitution of ongoing relationships.

In relation to neoliberal ideology, the key point here is that there are no strictly economic transactions. The money we use with one another is merely one form of what Graeber calls "social currency." As such, it should be used to "measure, assess, and maintain relationships between people, and only perhaps incidentally to acquire goods" (2014: 165). To remain true to any reasonable version of anthropological theory would require us to consider the strictly financial weight of any debt alongside other aspects of the relationships that exist between people. Basic human sociability requires that we "look past the question of individual or private ownership ... and at much more immediate and practical questions of who has access to what sorts of things and under what sorts of conditions" (2014: 165).

Of course, it is the case that these types of "practical" questions are quite difficult to answer when we are discussing relationships formed on a global scale. However, the default response cannot be a rigid adherence to the collection of poor nations' governmental debts by institutional lenders. The journalist Robert Kuttner, in a review of Graeber's book, gives the example of a rather obvious—and anthropologically sound—proposal by Anne O.

Krueger, an official appointed to the IMF in 2002 by US President George W. Bush. Under this proposal, nations overwhelmed by debt would be able to sue for bankruptcy within an international arena in the same manner as individuals or corporations can under national laws. According to Kuttner (2013), Krueger was "fairly shouted down by officials of the US Treasury and leading bankers." The austere discipline visited on the governments of poor countries is in stark contrast to the rights accorded to all matter of other economic entities.

Taking the nation-state as a key framework, the anthropologist Gustav Peebles has argued that credit and debt have "the capacity to integrate individuals with the corporate body that is the nation-state" (Peebles 2010: 34). It is precisely this type of integration that is missing when nation-states acquire sovereign debt. Anthropological analysis of the circulation of debt on a global basis should always ask *which* debtors are subject to *which* sorts of institutionalized integration. The fact that the sovereign debt of poor nations is treated as incapable of liquidation is the indication of a refusal, led by the governments of rich countries and transnational institutions such as the IMF, to establish meaningful relationships to accompany the movement of money.

Culture and Global Wealth

Drawing a comparison to the former system of official racial discrimination in South Africa, the political scientist Manfred Steger (2003: 135) has described the division between rich and poor countries as a "global apartheid." To put this division into perspective, it is first worthwhile to consider exactly how much wealth is at stake. Since the beginning of the Industrial Revolution, global economic wealth has undergone staggering growth. The scale of this growth can be seen in Figure 3.2, which charts the average global wealth per person over the past 3,000 years.

Also notable is what Gregory Clark (2007), the original author of this chart, calls the "Great Divergence." The huge explosion of wealth enjoyed by some has corresponded with the immiseration of others. Clark points out that many people in Africa have actually become poorer since the beginning of industrialization. Analyzed on a global basis, the core countries would seem not only to have grown on their own terms, but to actually have benefited at the expense of their poorest counterparts.

As it so happens, Clark also has an argument to go along with this chart. Because it is an argument about culture, it is of particular interest to anthropologists. For Clark, the best explanation of the great divergence involves the differing cultures of European and non-European nations. He specifically argues that factories in poor countries outside Europe have failed at imposing discipline on their workers and, thus, have failed to emerge as

36

Figure 3.2 Income per person, from 1000 BCE to 2000 CE. The year 1800 is equal to 1.
Source: Clark 2007: 2.

efficient sites for the investment of financial capital. His primary examples involve India and England.

Clark attributes the spread of industrial discipline in England to a set of highly particular demographic shifts. Specifically, he argues that large middle-class families during the eighteenth century passed the virtue of hard work down to their children, who further propagated the same values throughout English society as a whole. This demographic and cultural development ultimately allowed factory managers to direct workers in such a way as to implement efficient modes of production on the shop floor during the nineteenth century, creating the initial conditions for self-supporting economic growth.

Clark's argument has been forcefully rejected by other economic historians (see, for example, De Vries 2007), who note the very scant empirical evidence he uses to support his thesis. What is notable about this argument, however, and what has gained it considerable attention among economists, is the way that it uses culture to explain the origins of contemporary global inequality. According to Clark's account, what India lacked in comparison with England was a widespread culture of industrious work. It is only the achievement of this culture that allowed the initial impetus for industrialization.

A similarly culturalist argument has been offered by the economic historian Deirdre McCloskey (2010), who makes the case that it was the dignity afforded to entrepreneurs across European culture as a whole that served as the underlying cause for accelerating industrial growth during the nineteenth century. She argues that the situation in Europe at the beginning of the Industrial Revolution can be contrasted with that in other countries, where profit-seeking entrepreneurs were likely to be derided as greedy and self-interested. As one might suspect, McCloskey extends her argument to explain recent economic growth in China and India as the result of the dignity recently granted to entrepreneurs in those countries over the past several decades.

What is curious from an anthropological view is the way in which both of these economic historians treat the category of "culture." In each case, culture is attributed a causal role and is described as directly influencing economic growth.[4] Anthropologists, however, do not generally treat the notion of culture in this way. To begin with, it is unusual for an anthropologist to create a neat division between one set of behaviors labeled as cultural and one set of behaviors labeled as economic. For both Clark and McCloskey, economic regularities function independently from culture, except in the initial moment when market economies move toward unlimited capitalist accumulation. Furthermore, anthropologists do not generally argue that culture can be causal. Rather, the notion of culture is employed to describe the general forms of context which condition the overall constellation of human relationships. To return to the example furnished by McCloskey (2010), it seems just as plausible to say that economic growth in trade compels a newfound respect granted to entrepreneurs, rather than that the development of this respect strictly caused the growth in trade. Ultimately, every cultural situation involves forms of reinforcing and complex causality. The new culture of capitalism that emerged in the eighteenth and nineteenth century cannot be described in terms of a single precipitating event.

The foregoing concerns aside, what I find most difficult to accept about the sorts of explanation proposed by Clark and McCloskey is the way that they are predicated on the existence of distinct and fully coherent cultural groups. Indeed, Clark seems hardly to recognize that the two locations with which he is concerned—England and India—were deeply embroiled in a colonial relationship during the first creation of Indian factories. For him, this relationship is less important than the distinct national essence

---

4 McCloskey (2010) does try to complicate this view, protesting against "loose arguments for 'culture'" as the cause of economic growth (374), while nevertheless maintaining that obviously cultural forms of rhetoric were in fact "the greatest externalities" to explain economic growth (393–405), and even presenting this relationship as a mathematical equation (411).

that he attributes to these two nations. Indeed, this tendency toward essentialism is apparent in Clark's repeated eugenicist speculations, wherein he somewhat idly hypothesizes that the Industrial Revolution was the result of sexual selection for more industrious mates. This exceedingly unlikely evolutionary explanation is similar to his account of culture, insofar as the latter is predicated on the notion of cultural groups, which are presumed to be—in the words of James Ferguson and Akhil Gupta—"naturally disconnected" from one another rather than "hierarchically connected" (Gupta and Ferguson 1992: 8).

Gupta and Ferguson's advice is that anthropologists "rethink difference through connection"—that is, that we attempt to describe the sorts of differences that exist between England and India based on our understanding of how these places are interrelated. This same lesson could easily be applied to economic history, although historians such as Clark and McCloskey steadfastly avoid doing so. It should also be clear that any *divisions* between distinct groups are secondary to the *relationships* that anthropologists and other social scientists are capable of finding between those groups. After all, what is the point of even describing "England" and "India" unless we already understand these two concepts to be interrelated in some way? According to this sort of account, industrial capitalism emerged not as a result of the actions of a certain strictly separate cultural groups, but rather out of an encompassing network of relationships that helped to define those groups themselves.

Of course, the kind of thinking on display here by Clark and McCloskey is by no means limited to economic historians. The types of neoliberal ideology I describe above are inevitably "one size fits all" styles of thinking, in the sense that a neoliberal ideology requires interconnected groups to be imagined as strictly distinct entities. Once rich and poor countries are imagined as distinct examples of nation-states, it is easy to imagine that the same policies that work to the advantage of rich countries can also work to the advantage of poor countries. Unsurprisingly, the liberalizing reforms generally associated with neoliberalism (the sale of state-owned industries, the reduction of internal taxes and external tariffs, the loosening of labor market and consumer regulations, etc.) can therefore be presented as the only possibility for poor countries to become richer. The journalist Martin Wolf gives us an unusually candid example of this kind of blinkered vision:

> What the successful countries all share is a move towards the market economy, one in which private property rights, free enterprise and competition increasingly took the place of state ownership, planning and protection. They chose, however haltingly, the path of economic liberalization and international integration. This is the heart of the matter. All else is commentary. (quoted in Wade 2006: 106)

In defining the "heart of the matter," Wolf takes for granted that the world can be seen only as a series of individual countries, and that each individual country can benefit from liberal policies in basically the same way. The real question is not whether certain policies have helped certain countries, but whether globalization as an entire process is to the benefit of the world's poorest people, who happen to be concentrated in poor countries. On this question, the empirical economic literature does not provide anything like Wolf's conclusion. Globalization has not offered any clear economic benefits to the world's poorest people (Goldberg and Pavcnik 2007).

40

Availing ourselves of even the most generic anthropological worldview, it would perhaps be best to point out the stakes of liberalization in the following way: more liberal policies constitute a *risk* for people living in poor countries, but they constitute an *opportunity* for the primarily foreign investors seeking to profit from new kinds of industrial production in those countries. If local investments of capital succeed, then investors will improve their financial situation through profits while the local population improves its situation through the receipt of wages. However, if local investments by foreign capital fail, investors almost always have enough resources to walk away and invest elsewhere, while local participants have no choice but to remain in place and suffer the consequences. When neoliberal policy reforms fail, local inhabitants must deal alone with the attendant consequences of unemployment and eroding public services.[5]

We can sum up the main conclusions of this section in the following way: Neoliberal ideology encourages the recognition of disconnected national economies and the implementation of reforms that are suited to those theoretically individual entities. But in a world that is severely divided between core and peripheral countries, the risks involved in the blanket imposition of neoliberal reforms are asymmetrical. It is this asymmetrical relationship between rich and poor countries—and not the isolated performance of individual countries—that is crucial for anthropological analysis.

---

5 See cases mentioned in note 2 above.

CHAPTER 4

THE PRODUCTION OF INEQUALITY

As I discuss with reference to specific examples below, inequality is an *intersectional* phenomenon, meaning that it occurs in reinforcing and overlapping ways. To borrow an example from the work of Lisette Josephides (1985) discussed in the first chapter, gender inequality and economic inequality among the Kewa are largely overlapping—it is largely women who are economically exploited, and the economically exploited are largely women. Indeed, these two distinct forms of inequality are reinforcing, in the sense that gender identities provide an ideological justification for economic inequality, and economic inequality drives people to think in terms of gendered difference.

For these reasons, anthropological discussions of inequality are highly synthetic—they require that different kinds of information be combined into a single understanding. In the text below, I therefore put forth a set of analytically distinct issues that are initially described individually but which are to be synthesized together in the end:

- First, I describe *gender inequality* from a global perspective, arguing for the existence of emergent forms of global patriarchy.
- Second, I describe *economic inequality* as it is conditioned by capitalist economic relationships.
- Third, I attempt to relate this economic inequality occasioned by capitalism to *inequalities in political power* within nation-states.
- Fourth, I attempt to describe how these and other sorts of inequalities present in the contemporary world can be described as *intersecting* and *reinforcing* one another, particularly on a global scale.

Gender Inequality: Local and Global Concerns

As in the Kewa case described above, my first example involves gender inequality. It is worthwhile to begin by noting some of the astonishing statistics that have been compiled by scholars of women and globalization.

> It is evident from the facts and figures that 98 per cent of wealth on Earth is in the hands of men, and only 2 per cent belongs to women; the 225 richest "persons" in the world, who are men, own the same capital as the 2,500 million poorest people. Of these 2,500 million poorest people, 80 per cent are women but USD 780,000 million are spent on armaments worldwide compared to USD 12,000 million spent on women's reproductive health. In terms of child prostitution, 90 per cent are girls and 100 per cent of the beneficiaries are men. This is the unobtrusive and deadening condition of women in this era. (Dasgupta 2009: 243; see also Harrison 1997)

While these sorts of contemporary concerns cross disciplinary boundaries, the pervasive inequality between women and men across cultures is something that was noticed by anthropologists long before "globalization" itself became a buzzword.

In a passage quoted in Chapter 1, the anthropologist Sherry Ortner puts the issue this way: "The secondary status of woman in society is one of the true universals, a pan-cultural fact. Yet within that universal fact, the specific cultural conceptions and symbolizations of woman are extraordinarily diverse and even mutually contradictory. Further, the actual treatment of women and their relative power and contribution vary enormously from culture to culture, and over different periods in the history of particular cultural traditions. Both of these points—the universal fact and the cultural variation—constitute problems to be explained" (Ortner 1974: 67).

Ortner argues that discrimination against women is a "cultural universal" produced by the specifically symbolic association between women and nature. By the same token, she argues that this discrimination is not a universal biological fact based on the physiologic character of male and female humans. Contrary to Ortner's thesis, some anthropologists have argued that true gender equality does exist in some societies; however, these are at best isolated cases (see Rosaldo, Lamphere, and Bamberger 1974).

The prevalence of discrimination against women matters a great deal for globalization. It is worthwhile noting that there do exist examples of how the trend toward globalization can disrupt patriarchal values on the local level (Josephides's later work [1999] among younger Kewa villagers is an example of this). However, there is also a clear tendency for globalization to reinforce local forms of gender discrimination. In at least some cases, globalization would appear to operate by combining and reinforcing forms of gender discrimination that exist in separate local communities.

To understand how this can be so, it is helpful to look at an ethnographic case laid out by the sociologist Rhacel Salazar Parreñas (2001, 2008; see also Constable 2007). This case involves the mass emigration of Filipina women to Europe, North America, and other countries in Asia. Parreñas's ethnography concentrates on migrant women who serve as domestic workers in the homes of more affluent families in the more wealthy countries of Italy and the United States. She notes how migrant domestic servants are hidden from public view, away from one another and their home community. The immediate result of this is that migrant women suffer a certain kind of social isolation. The more cumulative result, however, is that migrant women working in domestic settings have few opportunities to organize themselves for better wages or political power. The possibilities for abuse in this sort of situation are substantial; Parreñas documents substandard wages, poor living conditions, and extreme demands by employers on their domestic servants. Even more prevalent, however, is the expectation that migrant women will gladly perform the sort of "care work" that inevitably accompanies domestic labor. Nannies and housekeepers are expected to care for the families they serve, sacrificing their own well-being for the well-being of growing children and busy parents. In the terms provided by the anthropologist Elana Buch (who has also undertaken an ethnography of paid domestic labor), "the value of women—historically constructed as 'natural' caregivers—is measured by their willingness and ability to subjugate their bodies and deny themselves bodily pleasure to meet the expectations and desires of others" (Buch 2013: 647).

It is not merely the expectations embedded in the local communities to which domestic laborers are "pulled" that affect the lives of these workers; women are also "pushed" from their home communities by highly gendered social forces. Here is how the journalist Barbara Ehrenreich and the sociologist Arlie Russell Hochschild explain further research by Parreñas and others, discussing the larger global dynamic of domestic labor migration:

> By migrating, a woman may escape the expectation that she care for elderly family members, relinquish her paycheck to a husband or father, or defer to an abusive husband. Migration may also be a practical response to a failed marriage and the need to provide for children without male help. In the Philippines, contributor Rhacel Salazar Parreñas tells us, migration is sometimes called a "Philippine divorce." And there are forces at work that may be making the men of poor countries less desirable as husbands. . . . Many female migrants, including those in Michele Gamburd's chapter in this volume, tell of unemployed husbands who drink or gamble their remittances away.

Notes one study of Sri Lankan women working as maids in the Persian Gulf: "It is not unusual … for the women to find upon their return that their Gulf wages by and large have been squandered on alcohol, gambling and other dubious undertakings while they were away. (Ehrenreich and Hochschild 2003: 10–11)

What we see, then, is that gender discrimination compels women from poor countries to migrate into domestic service jobs in rich countries, whereupon they are likely to meet yet another form of gender discrimi-
44   nation. Once they are in a position to send remittances home, they find that gendered forms of consumption have corrupted their ability to save or provide for people other than the men in their lives.

In this case, we can consider globalization as the merger, through the transnational migration of women, of what Parreñas (2008: 46) has referred to as "multiple patriarchies." This merger would appear to cement gendered forms of inequality in both the home and the target community of migrant domestic workers. We thus have two relatively distinct local forms of gender discrimination reinforcing one another to create a recognizably global form of patriarchy.

It might be easy to dismiss gender as a factor in globalization here, since the same migrations also have a clear economic logic. The global patriarchy I have sketched here is also part of a division between rich and poor countries (both of which include both men and women, of course). As Ehrenreich and Hochschild (2003: 8) point out, a Filipina domestic worker in Hong Kong can expect to earn 15 times the amount of a schoolteacher back home in the Philippines. But while the economic motivations involved are clear, it is crucial to note that these motivations would not exist without a gendered framework. Remittances sent home by women and care work performed by women are conditioned on the existence of gendered identities.

Viewing global migration through a strictly economic, gender-neutral lens therefore limits our ability to understand key aspects of the topic. In light of these types of concerns, the anthropologist Carla Freeman (2001) has argued that the impact of globalization on women is easy to ignore because gender discrimination also affects how globalization is studied. She points out that the vast trends in economic globalization can offer "masculinist grand theories of globalization that ignore gender as an analytical lens" (1008) to engage in an ostensibly gender-neutral historical process.

Capital and Economic Inequality

In a recent book on economic inequality, the economist Thomas Piketty has argued that the history of economic inequality for the past two centuries has been chaotic and unpredictable, affected not only by economic phenomena, but all manner of social divisions and historical events: "The history of inequality has not been a long, tranquil river. There have been many twists and turns and certainly no irrepressible, regular tendency towards a 'natural' equilibrium" (Piketty 2014: 274). In spite of this, he also emphasizes that there are certain economic forces that consistently bear on the formation of economic inequality.

These forces require only a few simple—and largely familiar—concepts to be explained. The first of these concepts is *capital*, which can be defined as wealth that is invested in the production of economic goods with the aim of generating a profit. Not all capital investments are successful, but a successful capitalist is someone who is able to consistently make money on investments. Today, it turns out that being a successful capitalist is usually not very difficult, since it is possible to invest small amounts of capital in many different private corporations, as well as to lend capital in exchange for interest to government bond sellers and others. The much greater trick, of course, is to have capital in the first place.

The second important concept in Piketty's analysis is the notion that *all the income that people receive can be divided, by definition, between income earned as wages and income earned from investment.* In the rich, industrialized countries, income from labor has generally been between two-thirds and three-quarters of all income, while the remaining one-third or one-quarter of total income has been from investments. From the point of view of production, this means that for every dollar's worth (or euro's worth, yen's worth, etc.) of economic value created by a person in any of the countries included in Piketty's analysis, 67 to 75 cents are returned to the laborer as wages and the remainder is returned to capitalist investors as profits.

Third, and finally, Piketty's analysis requires us to understand that *economies grow over time.* Until the advent of industrialization, growth rates were generally less than 1 per cent. Over the last two centuries, however, substantially higher growth rates have compounded to create the vast wealth that surrounds us today. Taking national economies as a convenient unit of analysis, Piketty makes the crucial point that economic growth actually helps to offset the production of economic inequality. As long as the rate of growth in the economy as a whole remains higher than the rate of profit, the growth of income from wages can keep up with the growth of income from capital. Unfortunately, this is not usually the case. Piketty (2014: 571) points to the fact that "wealth accumulated in the past grows more rapidly than output and wages"—the "central contradiction of capitalism." Piketty's metaphorical expression of this situation is poignant: "The entrepreneur inevitably tends to become a rentier, more and more dominant over those who own nothing but their labor. Once constituted, capital reproduces itself faster than output increases. The past devours the future" (571). In a well-known turn of phrase, the result is an

45

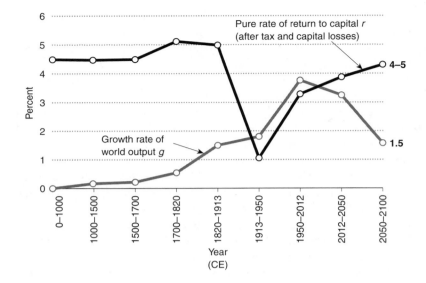

Figure 4.1 Annual rate of return vs. annual growth rate at the world level, Antiquity–2100.

Source: Piketty and Saez 2014: 841.

increasing *concentration of wealth*. The only thing that can counteract this concentration is a high rate of growth, which has the simple effect of creating more wealth to divide.

Given this analysis, it is immensely important to know whether or not economic growth is higher or lower than the rate of profit at any given point in time. Figure 4.1 depicts the actual historical relationship of the rate of growth (*g*) and the rate of profit (*r*) as compiled by Piketty and his collaborator Emmanuel Saez (2014).

Piketty and Saez (2014) conclude that the two millennia of human history leading up to roughly 1913 saw economic forces that pushed dramatically in the direction of economic inequality. It was the cataclysm of the two world wars that changed this trend, causing profit rates to temporarily plunge. During the same period, economic growth increased on a massive scale, temporarily eclipsing the rate of profit. The result was a short period of growing economic equality, notably to the benefit of the well-off middle classes of industrialized countries such as Canada and the United States. At the current juncture, however, Piketty and Saez see the world plunging again into growing economic inequality, as profit rates return to their historical norms and the economic growth that began with industrialization inevitably slows. If their analysis is correct, then countries with well-developed capitalist economies will face an unchecked flood of economic inequality in the years to come. Barring any further interventions, growing economic inequality within industrialized nations will be the "new normal" to which we must all become accustomed.

Democracy, Politics, and the Production of Inequality

Piketty's (2014) argument is different from the kind of neoliberal economic arguments described in the previous chapter, particularly since he depends primarily on data about historical trends rather than on a strictly formal model of rational decision-making by isolated individuals. Nevertheless, and in spite of his protestations that his work is as much historical as economic, Piketty maintains the methodological assumption that the economy simply operates on its own, without anything but automatic input by individual people. The crux of the issue here is that while Piketty wishes to see reforms enacted that would minimize inequality, he still treats the existence of capital as an inevitable fact. Because of this, he is willing to accept the minimum degree of inequality that is necessary for the reproduction of capitalism: "I have no interest in denouncing inequality or capitalism per se—especially since social inequalities are not in themselves a problem as long as they are justified, that is, 'founded upon common utility,' as article 1 of the 1789 Declaration of the Rights of Man and Citizen proclaims" (Piketty 2014: 7).

As I have sought to maintain from the beginning of this book, inequality is a problem in and of itself. In this sense, there are no perfect justifications for inequality, only more or less compellingly expedient ones. What we see here from Piketty is a pronounced willingness to abstain from critiquing capitalism, one which is offered precisely on pragmatic grounds. However, the terms that Piketty uses to justify inequality seem themselves problematic. The notion that inequality can be justified according to "common utility" suggests that there is a fair and transparent political process capable of deciding what that common utility is. What this further suggests is that we might begin to strive for equality in general by first establishing an egalitarian political community, one in which everyone is equally capable of deciding what is and is not a valued good. The work of liberal philosophers such as John Rawls also depends on this sort of assumption of an egalitarian political community capable of making decisions about degrees of economic equality (Rawls 1971).

Particularly when economic inequality is rampant, it is difficult to accept this priority for political equality. A recent line of inquiry in political science has helped to show precisely how corrosive economic inequality is to fair processes of political decision-making. I am referring in particular to the edited volume *Remaking America: Democracy and Public Policy in an Age of Inequality*. Looking at social welfare policy and the political life of the United States, the editors of this volume argue that inequality is not simply reproduced on an economic level. Rather, governmental policies that encourage the growth of inequality make future attempts to address inequality through public policy more difficult. They are particularly concerned about the rise of an "aggressive, well-organized and politically powerful conservative movement" that has leveraged the concentration of wealth in the United States and "weakened the voice of ordinary citizens on economic issues" to better guard the interests of the rich (Hacker, Soss, and Mettler 2007: 11, 13).

48   Two contributors to the above volume, Jacob S. Hacker and Paul Pierson, have jointly authored a popular book entitled *Winner-Take-All Politics: How Washington Made the Rich Richer—and Turned Its Back on the Middle Class.* They quote from a long list of philosophers and theorists (Plato, Aristotle, Plutarch, Tocqueville, Montesquieu, and Paine) to the effect that economic inequality tends to undermine democratic governance. Looking at the American political scene today, Hacker and Pierson conclude the following:

> The foremost obstacle to sustained reform is the enormous imbalance
> in organizational resources between the chief economic beneficiaries
> of the status quo and those who seek to strengthen middle-class
> democracy. Powerful groups defending the winner-take-all economy—
> business coalitions, Wall Street lobbyists, medical industry players—are
> fully cognizant of the massive stakes involved, and they are battle-
> ready after years of training. Vigilant and highly skilled at blocking
> or diverting challenges, these organized forces possess big advantages
> over the disorganized. On rare occasions, a vibrant politics of renewal
> emerges. If the momentum or attentiveness of reformers flags, however,
> opponents are fully capable of snatching victory from the jaws of
> defeat. (Hacker and Pierson 2011: 291)

It is precisely the inability of democratic institutions to address economic inequality that calls into question Piketty's insistence that inequality is not in and of itself a problem and that "if we are to regain control of capitalism, we must bet everything on democracy." To directly counter Piketty's point, I would say that if we are to gain control of our democracies, we must be willing to commit ourselves, without reservations, to solving the problem of inequality.

Intersectionality and the Production of Inequality

The minimal conclusion to take from this chapter is that various types of gendered, economic, and political inequality exist. However, we have also begun to see how these forms of inequality can intersect. We have seen how gender and economic inequality are interrelated for Kewa women and for women who are migrant workers. We have also seen, directly above, how economic and political inequality are interrelated. Obviously, there are many more forms of inequality that could be described in a similar fashion. Moreover, we can expect the intersections between forms of inequality to multiply as we explore increasing numbers of forms of inequality. In the final section of this chapter, I want to suggest how we might begin to understand the basic fact that different forms of inequality intersect.

A good example to begin with involves the historical research of the anthropologist Karen Brodkin (1998), who has looked closely at one example of the relationship between ethnic discrimination and capitalist production. **49** Looking at the garment industry in New York City around 1900, Brodkin shows how labor unions dominated by British, German, and Irish immigrant communities managed to exclude Jewish immigrants from trades such as construction, printing, and transportation. This exclusion left large numbers of Jewish workers eager to take up any job they could, fueling the growth of low-skill jobs in the garment industry. Brodkin's conclusion is that the production of clothing in sweatshops involved the exploitation of a large labor force with low skills, and that the formation of this labor force was aided by ethnic discrimination against Jews. In a parallel case, Brodkin describes the ongoing racial stigmatization of Mexican workers in the United States. Her broader conclusion concerns the "ethno-racial" mapping of the US labor force, a process with very broad and very diffuse results.

Labor historians, including Sonya Rose (1988), have noted similar patterns of discrimination against women workers, who were frequently excluded from the "labor aristocracy" of high-paying union jobs. Carla Freeman (2000), an anthropologist whose work has already been mentioned above, has similarly noted the way that gender identities have contributed to a "pink-collar" workforce in the Caribbean. According to the sociologist Leslie McCall (2001), attempts to understand such cases require an understanding of "complex inequality" as it involves the intersection of different class-based, racial, and gender identities. McCall shows, for example, how the transformation of the US economy in the direction of more high-technology production has effects that are uniquely stratified by class (i.e., the loss of moderately skilled jobs and the growth of the working poor) and by gender (i.e., pervasive discrimination against women in highly skilled, high-tech occupations).

The results of these sorts of intersections are several. First, it can be difficult to say which sorts of inequality are at play in which cases. Forms of economic exploitation might coincide, for example, with discriminatory treatment of women by men at their place of work. We cannot simply label such cases as instances of economic inequality or gender inequality—they are both. Second, it is necessary to understand how discernably different forms of inequality can reinforce one another. This sort of reinforcement can sometimes take surprising forms. In recent years, a series of authors has brought attention to the notion of *homonationalism*. According to the women's studies scholar Jasbir Puar, who coined the term, there has been a tendency in recent years to make judgments about racialized others according to those others' views on gay rights, as when countries in the Islamic world are treated as inherently backward based on the presence of homophobia within their borders: "The narrative of progress for gay rights is thus built on the backs of racialized and sexualized others, for whom such progress was either once achieved but is now backsliding or has yet to arrive. This process relies on the shoring up of the respectability of homosexual subjects in relation to the performative reiteration of the pathologized perverse (homo- and hetero-) sexuality of racial others, specifically Muslim others, upon whom Orientalist and neo-Orientalist projections are cast" (Puar 2013: 337).

Puar (2011) has pointed in particular to the attempt by Israeli governmental officials and Israeli nationalists to justify the occupation of Palestine based on the Israeli government's superior defense of gay rights. For Puar, this "pinkwashing" is an intolerable attempt to justify one form of inequality (i.e., the political repression of stateless Palestinians by Israeli military occupiers) by appealing to a guarantee of equal treatment of a different group of people (i.e., some subset of gay people living in Israel), especially insofar as it draws on racialized and sexualized stereotypes of Palestinians as inherently backward and other.

The foregoing is a clear example of intersectionality, although it is not a clear-cut case of direct reinforcement of two distinct forms of inequality. It seems to me that the lesson to draw from Puar's analysis of homonationalism and pinkwashing is that the intersection of inequalities does not always mean their direct reinforcement. When one form of equality is used to justify a different form of inequality, we have a more complex case of contradiction. As it so happens, the two groups of people in question do not generally overlap—by definition, gay people living in Israel are not also living in Palestine.[1] Still, the end result is not only individual forms of inequality reproduced by themselves, but of complex, overlapping, and sometimes contradictory inequalities producing one another.

---

[1] Homonationalist thinking can also be used to justify forms of discrimination that are weaker than those perceived in other countries. At the time of this writing, a US senator was quoted in the press as justifying discriminatory legislation against queer people in the following way: "But I also think it's important that we have a sense of perspective about our priorities. In Iran, they hang you for the crime of being gay."

CHAPTER 5

RIGHTS, EQUALITY, AND THE NATION-STATE

The last several decades have seen a huge growth in attempts by anthropologists to understand how people encounter both national cultures and state power. The result is that the nation-state as an institution looms large in contemporary anthropology. In the terms offered by the anthropologist Arjun Appadurai (1996: 198), the sorts of "situated communities" preferred by ethnographers are increasingly subject to the "context-producing drives of more complex hierarchical organizations, especially those of the nation-state." The existence of nation-states is particularly relevant to the topic of inequality, since they are frequently organized in relation to various forms of political and economic equality.

In this chapter, I am concerned with political equality within nation-states. Several points about this should be made at the outset:

- Forms of political equality within nation-states are highly various. The most liberal nations in the world—who are generally also the richest—tend to hold political equality as a kind of ultimate good, situating it even as the bedrock of political community. Political leaders and the leaders of nongovernmental organizations in these same rich nations are frequently critical of authoritarian violations of political equality that occur in less well-off countries.
- Political equality, although often held up as an ideal, is never perfect. As I already hinted at in the previous chapter, even the most liberal nation-states do not allow for an equal distribution of political power. Wealth and status play an important—even essential—role in the formation of political life.

- Finally, the dominant conception relevant to political equality in the world today is that of *rights*. To speak of a right is to assert a basic form of political power meant to be shared by all. Obviously, real life is not so uniform that each situation relevant to each person within a given nation-state can be easily described in relation to a particular set of rights. Rather, anthropologists have generally been concerned with "rights talk" as a form of discourse that guides ordinary political understanding and is frequently imposed by governments as much as rights themselves are heeded by them.

In the text below, I discuss some examples of rights talk and explore some of the most important limitations on political equality in the world today. Before I do this, however, it is worthwhile to briefly explain why political equality within nation-states is an important topic to address in relation to specifically global forms of inequality. To begin with, we should be clear on the fact that globalization has actually strengthened nation-states. The sociologist Jean-François Bayart (2004: 466) has argued, along these lines, that the nation-state is the "product and not the victim of globalization." Even the reduction in tariffs and the "harmonization" of policies discussed in Chapter 3 presuppose the existence of strong national institutions capable of maintaining and enforcing transnational agreements.[1]

Globalization strengthens nation-states, but nation-states also play a tremendously large role in defining global relationships. As I discuss in more detail below, the most important paradigm for political identity in the world today involves the notion of the *citizen*. With the exception of the rather metaphorical notion of the "global citizen," to be a citizen means to be the member of an individual nation. In this sense, it remains completely unclear what it might mean to talk about political equality across national borders. Our best indications about the possibilities for global political equality come from examples of rights talk and, to coin a phrase, "citizenship talk" on the national level.

Globalization, the Nation-State, and "Rights Talk"

Anthropologists have had few qualms about rejecting economic individualism. As should be clear from various topics discussed in the first several

---

1   The one partial exception to this is the European Union (EU), which increasingly operates as a kind of supernation, or a federation of nations. Even at the time of this writing, however, the "European project" threatens to founder due to nationalist forces. Relatively poor countries in the EU are threatened by unemployment and spiraling sovereign debt, while relatively rich countries in the EU refuse to take part in a shared solution to these problems. Indeed, the resolution of these difficulties appears to demand one of two paths—either the emergence of genuine European statehood ("the United States of Europe") or a return to a political landscape similar to that prior to the institutionalization of the EU.

chapters of this book, the notion that the world is ultimately made up of individual people, and that these people are defined by their economic interests, makes little sense for the discipline of anthropology. Economic anthropologists have been particularly clear in rejecting what James G. Carrier (1998: 2) has called the "abstract-economic world view." Trying to make sense of rational economic motivations, anthropologists have generally assigned interest-based rationality to a longer list of possible motivations. In a summary of the basic conclusions that are shared by economic anthropologists, Sutti Ortiz (2006: 74) argues that "economic actors are just as concerned with their social standing, their identity and autonomy as they are with maximizing utility or income in the conventional sense." One might add that economic actors are concerned with reciprocity and interdependence as much as they are with individual interests.

By contrast, anthropologists have been more ambivalent concerning the notion of political individualism. The notion that each person is an autonomous unit of political decision making may well be a part of a particular European intellectual heritage. Indeed, adherence to this notion does seem to require a peculiarly ideological vision of individual autonomy. Critics, such as Elizabeth Povinelli (2006: 156), have critiqued the notion of the "autological subject" as implying a "clean division … between individual freedom and social coercion," with the result that substantive forms of mistreatment are legitimated when they can be couched in the language of rights and political inclusion. Defenders of political rights, such as Terence Turner, have insisted that they are an important part of an "emancipatory cultural politics" capable of operating across nations and cultural groups.

This ambivalence about the value and importance of individual rights mirrors the complexities of rights talk as it has been uncovered by anthropologists working on the ground. A broad array of rights talk has been uncovered by Harri Englund during his fieldwork in Malawi. Surveying a variety of governmental agencies and nongovernmental advocates, Englund (2006: 47) begins with the notion that "contemplating human rights in the abstract is a luxury that only the most isolated occupants of the ivory tower can afford." He accordingly diagnoses rights talk as an elitist preoccupation, one that functions to guarantee the prestige of those educated elite not directly aligned with the government. Englund argues that civil society organizations that seek to enforce human rights throughout that country are largely ineffective in their efforts to better the lives of the poor, but that they do succeed in justifying their own existence by appealing to values shared by foreign donors. The end result is a deep, but largely invisible, complicity between those who campaign in the name of human rights and the more institutionally entrenched political elite associated with the state.

Matthew Engelke, an anthropologist whose fieldwork takes place in nearby Zimbabwe, points to similar problems. While labeling himself an

53

"anthropologist interested in human rights" and professing a concern for how specific individuals can be protected from unfair treatment through rights talk, Engelke admits that the notion of human rights can seem foreign for many of his informants. Engelke describes one informant's surprised reaction when he comes to understand that his homophobic assault on a foreigner has been framed as a violation of the assaulted person's human rights—"we wondered what human rights he was talking about," the perpetrator replies (quoted in Engelke 1999: 289). In at least this case, the discourse of human rights seems to lack a basic legitimacy. Engelke argues that a straightforward assessment that it is morally wrong to assault another person because of his sexual orientation is more consistent with local context than the more abstract assertion of a human rights violation. The ethnographer's conclusion (308): "In the long run the historical success of human rights activism, in Zimbabwe and elsewhere, will be judged in terms of an ability to stress the importance of the moral sentiments upon which the terms of human rights are based." Rights talk may be important in some instances, but it remains empty without some appeal to the embodied moral beliefs of the people involved.

Ambivalence about rights talk must also be considered in terms of neocolonial global relationships, within which the views associated with European and European-derived cultures are often given precedence. Describing the South African context, the legal scholar Thandabantu Nhlapo (2000: 148) argues that African and European cultures do not "enjoy equality of status" even within South Africa and that the danger therefore exists that "the dominant culture will be tempted to enlist the prestige of the international human rights movements to mask a basic intolerance of competing world views." Along similar lines, the historian Bonny Ibhawoh (2008: 2) has pointed out that "to exercise one's rights has come to be taken as something inherently good, an index of social and political progress." When rights are used as a symbol of modernity and progress, they necessarily exclude and discriminate against those who are understood to remain outside the forms of predominantly European culture that dominate in the modern world.

Inequality and Insurgent Citizenship in Brazil

One important aspect of Englund's work involves the insight that rights talk in Malawi is very often performed *by* the educated elite *on behalf of* the rural poor. As he has also pointed out in his book about call-in radio in Malawi (Englund 2011), more popular sorts of discourses about right and wrong are not necessarily couched in the language of rights. However, there are places in the world where popular political discourses do involve the notion of rights. As I have already noted, inherent in the notion of rights is the notion that they are borne equally by all people. For centuries, governments have typically granted full equality only to particular people (i.e., white men, and especially white men who owned land). In theory, however, the notion of rights means that *all* persons who inhabit a particular community have the same privileges and protections. Popular actors who are willing to take up this universalist claim are bound to be much more comfortable with rights talk than are the poor people at the center of Englund's ethnography.

Engaging with rights talk in this way means challenging political practices that advantage some and disadvantage others. Since the beginning of his fieldwork career in the late 1980s, the anthropologist James Holston has engaged with the gap between the universal guarantees of rights explicitly stated in the Brazilian constitution and the actual political and legal practices surrounding the exercise of rights in that country. His fieldwork has largely focused on the residents of a series of "autoconstructed" Brazilian neighborhoods, including Sobradinho (Holston 1991) in the city of Brasilia and Lar Nacional (Holston 2008) in the city of São Paulo. For the most part, these neighborhoods consist of homes that have been built without an official permit. Over the course of years and decades, places like these have slowly evolved from collections of bare shacks lining unfinished dirt roads to organized neighborhoods of completed brick houses joined together in an elaborate municipal infrastructure. Unfortunately, however, the land deeds acquired by residents of such autoconstructed neighborhoods have often later turned out to be contested or fraudulent. In some cases, entire neighborhoods have been built on the basis of fraudulent deeds that were illegally attained by *grileiros* (swindlers) and sold on to local residents.

The case of Lar Nacional, which is at the center of Holston's most recent ethnographic research, does not involve this sort of straightforward fraud. The residents of this neighborhood happen to have purchased the land on which they built their houses from someone with a legitimate, albeit imprecise, land claim. During the 1990s, a court ruled that this original land claim conflicted with a stronger such claim, and that the residents of Lar Nacional had unintentionally acquired pieces of land that actually belonged to a man named Humberto Reis Costa. In the wake of the court's decision, the residents of Lar Nacional were ordered to either surrender their homes to Reis Costa or negotiate the terms on which they could pay a second time for the land on which their houses were built. Both of these options would have been disastrous for the poor, working-class residents of the neighborhood.

As Holston shows, it is regularly the case that suits brought by rich Brazilians receive preferential treatment in Brazilian courts, particularly when it comes to land claims. In a context where these claims are frequently overlapping and imprecise, any doubts about ownership tend to be

55

resolved in favor of the wealthier, and therefore more powerful, party. Indeed, Holston argues that the land laws have actually been designed to be so complex as to ensure that those with more unofficial sway within the legal system will have a distinct advantage. This is the source of the popular Brazilian saying "For enemies, the law." Holding people to the letter of the law can be a potent weapon, particularly when one party to a disagreement does not have the resources or sway to effectively pursue the matter in court. Holston refers to this and related phenomena as the *misrule of law*. Under the misrule of law, the protections ostensibly granted to all actually function to ensure the special privileges enjoyed by elites alone. It is important to note that this situation is not the result of a single, intentional act, but rather of the slow evolution of laws in a context where the wealthy hold a great deal of sway over the political system.

From a somewhat general point of view, the misrule of law is an obvious problem: despite legal guarantees, poor people are unlikely to receive their due in court, and the complexity of the law actually serves as a hindrance to their ability to exercise their rights. From a more specific and human point of view, the tragedy in such cases is equally obvious: the residents of Lar Nacional made a good-faith effort to pay for the land under their homes, but were likely to be pushed aside by a justice system unequipped to hear their concerns. Whether or not there is a truly equitable resolution between Reis Costa and the residents of Lar Nacional is hard to say. It does seem clear, however, that many who are in a situation similar to that of Lar Nacional's residents are unlikely to even have a chance at such a resolution.

In spite of these unfortunate facts, Holston does not take a defeatist tone in his ethnography. Instead, he focuses on the way that residents of Lar Nacional have tried to fight back and retain their homes. Facing the shared threat of eviction and homelessness, the first thing they did was to band together to create an organization dubbed the Society of Friends of the Neighborhood (SAB) (Figure 5.1). Still in existence as of Holston's most recent publication, the SAB has the goal of fighting eviction and regularizing the land deeds held by residents of Lar Nacional. As Holston shows, even forming an organization such as the SAB is difficult, since individual homeowners are often scared of the powers that be and unwilling to band together to fight. Wealthy parties such as Reis Costa need only intimidate individual opponents into a disadvantageous settlement, whereas the residents of neighborhoods such as Lar Nacional must band together before they can even begin to fight. At best, membership in the SAB offered residents a protracted legal and political struggle, one that would require not only lawyers and courtroom appearances, but also arduous attempts to rally the press and local politicians to their side. Holston himself has been part of this struggle. True to the notion of an ethnographer as participant observer, Holston has volunteered at various times to do public relations

Figure 5.1 Lar Nacional protestors.
Source: Holston 2008: 297.

work on behalf of the SAB, and so has become intimately familiar with the residents of Lar Nacional as both an onlooker and a political ally.

After Humberto Reis Costa's death, his heirs continued their attempts to evict the residents of Lar Nacional. While the particulars of the various court cases involving the Reis Costa family and the residents of Lar Nacional are convoluted, what is most important for the argument presented by Holston is how the people of Lar Nacional have been able to fight the Reis Costa family to a stalemate on multiple occasions and have not simply had their interests pushed aside by biased or corrupt judges. This might seem like a minor victory, particularly given the guarantee in the Brazilian constitution that "all persons are equal before the law." As should be clear by now, however, Holston's ethnography is predicated not merely on the *theoretical* notion of equal treatment, but also on the *practical* fact that there has been a long history of legalized discrimination against poor people in Brazil.

According to Holston, the ability to actualize an egalitarian political community in Brazil today requires, above all, a group of people willing to take on the mantle of "insurgent citizenship." Being an insurgent citizen means learning to manipulate a political and legal system that is systematically biased toward the privileged and the wealthy. While judges have ruled at least twice that the residents of Lar Nacional must surrender their homes to Reis Costa or his heirs, the members of the SAB were successful on both occasions in delaying the implementation of the judicial decree. On the first occasion, lawyers for the SAB had the eviction decree overruled on a technicality. On the second occasion, the city government temporarily circumvented the eviction following favorable news coverage for the residents of Lar Nacional. For Holston, the ability of members of the SAB to assert themselves in the courts and to force the action of the city government are signs that working-class people have begun to acquire a genuinely first-class citizenship.[2]

58

The notion of insurgent citizenship is important to Holston because it seems to offer the people of Lar Nacional a way out of their predicament. Holston insists that there is great power in attempts by poor and working-class people to use rights talk in such a way as to maintain that they are equal members of a formal political community. Broadly characterizing the work of the SAB, he concludes that

> ... these struggles [to secure regular title to long-established house lots in Lar Nacional and other neighborhoods] have produced a broad expansion among the urban poor of the expectation that as citizens ... their problems can be addressed in terms of the rights and dignity of democratic citizenship rather than by other means, such as patronage, favor or revolution. (2008: 230)

One resident of Lar Nacional underlines the importance accorded by poor people of accessing the title of "citizen":

> A citizen was a guy, in the time of my parents, loaded with money. It's true. The citizen was the chic, the rich, the owner of a business. . . . The worker was not a citizen, no. That didn't exist. The worker was a peon

---

2 As mentioned in the first two chapters, historical context is particularly important here. Holston argues that the systematic misrule of law in Brazil has its roots in forms of legally sanctioned discrimination against freed slaves and indigenous people. In the case of its indigenous peoples, the Brazilian state has long considered "tribal specificity and indeed Indianness itself as a temporary condition" (2008: 71) that would be relieved by full integration into the nation, with the result that the state could own land on behalf of Indians as they ostensibly remained in the process of becoming incorporated into the nation as first-class citizens. At the same time, this process meant the denial of Indians' "autonomous culture" as an alternative basis for the exercise of power and privilege. Indian communities could not jointly hold land as communities, but only as individual citizens. Ultimately, this made the inclusion of indigenous citizens of Brazil equivalent to their "total domination" by paternalistic elites who chose when and how indigenous groups could occupy this or that piece of land. This version of *inegalitarian inclusion* set the groundwork for the appropriation of huge tracts of indigenous lands, first by local governments and then by private property holders. For Holston, this appropriation of native land helped to set the pattern for other abuses of land law by wealthy Brazilians.

[*peão*]. Peon, peon, peon, his whole life. My father came to São Paulo a simple sharecropper and died a simple construction worker. But he met all his obligations, all his duties. And when he went somewhere and needed some right, no one treated him as a citizen. They made him into a marginal, as if he were trash. I saw that and I experienced that too. The injustice made me furious. (quoted in Holston 2008: 255)

While there is little doubt that second-class treatment has always made people angry, what Holston is trying to show is that in Brazil, this anger is increasingly the basis for the effective organization of the "popular classes" in the form of an "organized participatory citizenry" (2008: 252; see also Wainwright 2003).

Holston also argues for a crucial relationship between the growing demands for first-class citizenship documented in his fieldwork and the electoral politics of contemporary Brazil. The election in 2003 of President da Silva (popularly known as "Lula") was seen by many Brazilians as a watershed. Born and raised in an "autoconstructed" urban neighborhood similar to Lar Nacional, Lula was seen as "a man who had triumphed without becoming elite, who had succeeded through his experience of the common, and who presented his individual success as expressly collective" (Holston 2008: 6). Holston further argues that "Lula won [his election] because Brazilians recognized in this common aspect of achievement the best possibility for remaking a nation rotted by the convergence of great wealth and grotesque inequality" (6).

These words constitute high praise from an anthropologist, whose research methods often require detachment and disinterest above enthusiasm and partisanship. Examined more closely, however, it is clear that Holston's praise is not actually for Lula himself, but instead for the people who elected him. Moreover, this praise is not for anything that these people have actually accomplished, but rather for the mere fact of recognizing themselves as citizens of equal standing. Holston is most impressed by those "laboring Brazilians" who "long for a share in their country's immense resources, forever monopolized by a habitually disparaging, pampered and immune elite who always seem relentlessly in control of Brazil's destiny" (2008: 6).

Citizenship and Illegality in the United States

It is quite clear from the previous section that the category of citizen has a special importance for the exercise of rights and the realization of formal equality within the nation-state. To be a *citizen* means to be a full member of a national community, one whose rights are universally shared with all other citizens. To be an *insurgent citizen* in the sense used by Holston is to insist that these rights be actually meaningful. But what about the category of citizenship itself? Would this category be an unequivocally good thing, as long as bias and the misrule of law could be prevented?

The main issue here involves the simple fact that the very category of the citizen is exclusionary—it implies the existence of some persons who are *not* citizens. Of course, this is primarily a concern for people who cross national borders to live in a place where they do not have citizenship. In a country such as the United States, there are millions of immigrants who are not citizens and yet take part in all aspects of daily life. Some of these immigrants have come to the United States with specific legal permission to work or study. Many of those who come to work in low-wage occupations, however, do not have this same official permission. These people are often referred to either as *undocumented workers* or *illegal immigrants*. In this case, however, the choice between these two terms can actually be quite important.

Let us consider these terms at face value:

- **Undocumented workers** would appear to be people who fulfill a legitimate economic function while remaining outside the system of registration that is officially necessary for employment.
- By contrast, **illegal immigrants** would appear to be those whose entire actions are by definition outside the law, whether they are working or not.

Given these two alternatives, the former provides a more apt description. While the act of crossing a border without permission is very often illegal, the work that most such immigrants do is, in and of itself, very obviously legitimate. For precisely this reason, the notion of the *illegal immigrant* cannot capture the legitimate functions of the work done by *undocumented workers*.

There is broad recognition of the importance of undocumented workers in the US economy, including on the part of business leaders. In a 2013 op-ed in the *Washington Post*, the CEO of the Marriot International hotel chain described how undocumented immigrants "fill jobs that Americans are unwilling or unable to fill." He went on to explain how "streamlining the legal channels for entering this country and joining the US workforce would provide a serious boost to productivity" (Sorenson 2013).

Undocumented workers play a particularly important role in the agricultural sector, where their work helps to directly keep food prices down for the consuming public at large. And while experts disagree about the precise economic impact of undocumented labor, what seems obvious is the more basic fact that undocumented immigrants in the United States produce and consume economic goods alongside citizens and documented immigrants and are, by virtue of this participation, a legitimate presence in the United States.

According to the anthropologist Nicholas De Genova, framing undocumented workers as "illegal immigrants" helps to establish a persistent cultural script of *illegality*. This script—that is, a way of talking and thinking that is common and taken for granted—helps to represent undocumented workers as a foreign and invasive presence (see Borneman 1986). By contrast, De Genova (2002: 424) insists on a different reality. He argues that migration does not simply involve the arrival of foreigners from outside the nation, but that it is actually a complex phenomenon "produced" by actors within the nation. Employers in the United States insistently seek out low-wage workers, and immigration laws that systematically prevent the legal entrance of low-wage workers to meet this demand will necessarily produce undocumented labor. To frame this process as specifically involving "illegal immigration" is to **61** absolve the employers and lawmakers who participate in producing undocumented labor of their part in this process. One might note, for example, that one never hears the terms *illegal employers* (those who employ undocumented workers) or *illegal consumers* (those who benefit from undocumented work). In this vein, De Genova argues (422) that "undocumented migrations would be inconceivable were it not for the value they produce through the diverse services they supply to citizens."

De Genova argues that what the category of illegality does serve to do is consign undocumented migrants to a subservient status, one in which their everyday existence is particularly insecure. Following the earlier work of Susan Bibler Coutin (2003), he points to the way that charities, college admissions officers, local police, and social welfare agencies are increasingly responsible for vetting the immigration status of individual persons. On this account, the cultural practices surrounding "illegality" help to produce a net of surveillance surrounding undocumented workers throughout their everyday life.

Several scholars have expanded upon De Genova's highly cited arguments about illegality as a cultural script. Among these scholars is the sociologist Roberto G. Gonzales. In his work, Gonzales gives a particularly compelling account of what it means for the children of undocumented workers to come of age in a country where they are also denied full official membership:

> For undocumented youth, the transition into adulthood is accompanied by a transition into illegality that sets them apart from their peers. Undocumented youngsters share a confusing and contradictory status in terms of their legal rights and the opportunities available to them. On the one hand, because of the Supreme Court ruling in *Plyler v. Doe* (1982), they have the legal right to a K to 12 education. Furthermore, the Family Educational Rights and Privacy Act prevents schools from releasing any information from students' records to immigration authorities, making school a protected space in which undocumented status has little to no negative effect. On the other hand, undocumented young adults cannot legally work, vote, receive financial aid, or drive in most states, and deportation remains

a constant threat. Unauthorized residency status thus has little direct impact on most aspects of childhood but is a defining feature of late adolescence and adulthood and can prevent these youth from following normative pathways to adulthood. (2011: 605)

Around the time they graduate from high school, undocumented youth face a stark reckoning: there is a place for them in US society—but only as children. All the ordinary prerequisites of adult life remain out of reach. Many of these young people have parents who have labored over years or decades as undocumented workers, hoping that their own children would not suffer the same fate.

While the debate over labor immigration is hotly contested, what is crucial to notice in this context is the clear political inequality between citizens on the one hand and undocumented workers and their children on the other. These two groups of people exist side by side, and are indeed economically dependent on one another, but the law grants them each a fundamentally different status. We might think of the category of citizen as involving guarantees of formal equality, in the sense that each person who holds the status of citizen is seen to be formally similar to all others. In this case, however, we can see rather clearly how the category of citizen helps to establish a very overt and formal *in*equality between residents who have the status of citizen and those who do not.

In recent years, Latinos in the United States have been at the center of a movement for immigration reform, and thus for greater formal equality between citizens and noncitizens. This movement reached its height in 2006, when millions marched to protest pending legislation that would have substantially increased the instances of deportation of undocumented immigrants. This legislation ultimately failed, and the widespread protest movement in support of greater equality for undocumented immigrants largely dissipated as a result. However, related protests have continued in a somewhat reduced form, particularly in connection with so-called DREAM legislation, which is designed to ensure that undocumented youth are able to find a path to citizenship or permanent legal residency once they become adults.[3] For those undocumented immigrants who came to the United States as young children and see themselves as fully and solely American, there is nothing more important for them than their ability to maintain residency and work without the threat of deportation.

Undocumented immigrants ultimately face a structural problem: although they participate every day in the life of the nation, the nation itself is defined in opposition to them. In this context, it is worth mentioning

---

3 "DREAM" is said by proponents of this legislation to stand for *D*evelopment, *R*elief, and *E*ducation for *A*lien *M*inors.

that there are some very sensible and immediate ways in which the lives of undocumented immigrants could be improved. To begin with, the US government could seek out and prosecute the *employers* who hire undocumented immigrants (often at exploitative wages and under harsh or illegal conditions) rather than the immigrants themselves. Granting amnesty (i.e., freedom from prosecution and the ability to apply for citizenship) to those workers who are clearly productive members of American society would also be helpful. Whatever one makes of these or any other policies, however, what is most notable from an anthropological perspective is the way that the category of citizen can help to provide for formal *in*equality as much as for formal equality.

CHAPTER 6

WELFARE AND ECONOMIC INEQUALITY

In the previous chapter, we saw some of the ways that people struggle for political equality within the nation-state. In this chapter, I consider how the nation-state framework is also important to the distribution of economic wealth and thus to the existence of economic inequality. My primary concern is with the welfare state.

Before I begin to discuss this topic, however, it is worth considering the ways in which political *equality* and economic *inequality* can become entangled. In the previous chapter, I characterized liberal regimes as being particularly concerned with political equality, especially as it concerns the notions of rights and citizenship. However, the liberal tradition has long held that equality is not simply a matter of persons, but also of property. Since the seventeenth century, liberal theorists have consistently held that the duty of governments is to protect each person as well as "his whole property" (John Locke). Of course, an explicit defense of private property also functions as an implicit defense of economic inequality. In today's world, the protection of private property inevitably leads to the accumulation of capital and thus the sort of self-reinforcing economic inequality described in Chapter 4.

It is even possible to look on political equality as a key form of support for economic inequality, since the rights-bearing individual described in the previous chapter can also be framed as the "possessive individual" (Macpherson 1962) whose private ownership of property trumps the needs of others. This very basic institutional arrangement is by no means universal, but because it is associated both with the wealthiest nation-states and the transnational organizations that those nations support (see Chapter 3), it is an extremely important feature of the contemporary world. To put the point succinctly, the liberal nation-state is *hegemonic* in the contemporary transnational order.

Although severely limited in its ability to actually redistribute wealth, the welfare state stands out as an institution closely aligned with the liberal nation-state, yet generally dedicated to ameliorating the worst effects of inequality under capitalism. As I suggest in this chapter, certain aspects of the welfare state can systematically encourage inegalitarian attitudes by allowing welfare beneficiaries to be demonized. What is most notable on a systematic basis, however, is that the most egalitarian countries in the world have robust welfare states. These countries have succeeded—at least more so than others—in creating economic solidarity through the provision of public social services.

At least in the short term, welfare states based within individual nations are the best hope for improving economic inequality. This chapter is there-fore arranged as a tour of the possibilities and limitations inherent in the welfare state.

Welfare and Economic Inequality in South Africa

Welfare states are frequently associated with rich countries, but middle-income countries are also increasingly host to broad welfare programs. South Africa provides a particularly interesting example because of the dramatic transformations of political equality it experienced several decades ago. The end of South African apartheid in 1994 was greeted as a global event of the first order. A century and a half of colonialism followed by 50 years of officially sanctioned legal discrimination against black South Africans came to a halt with the election of Nelson Mandela—a long-standing leader of the African National Congress (ANC)—as the first black president of South Africa. Mandela would go on to be an important symbol of civil rights and freedom from racist domination in Africa and throughout the world.

What has been most striking about post-apartheid South Africa, how-ever, is not the political liberation of the black majority, but rather the continued existence of dire economic inequalities, especially between black and white people. Today, most black South Africans live under material con-ditions that are equally horrendous to those they suffered under apartheid. High crime, low levels of educational achievement, dilapidated housing and infrastructure, and high unemployment are the rule of the day for the more than 10 million black South Africans who live in extreme poverty.

This state of affairs contrasts starkly with the pledge of economic equal-ity made by the ANC and other anti-apartheid organizations starting in the 1950s. The Freedom Charter, a document signed by a variety of these organizations in 1957, criticized the economic exploitation of black South

Africa, arguing that "the system of White supremacy has its roots in the cheap labor need of the major economic groups of the country." This same document went on to propose that the substantive disadvantage of black South Africans should be ended with the transfer of mineral wealth, banks, and "monopoly industries" from private hands to a new South African government that included the black majority. In short, the ANC and its allies called for a form of democratic socialism that both included the black majority as full citizens and allowed for a far greater degree of economic equality through the state's ownership of key industries.

Unfortunately for the proponents of this plan, the end of apartheid 67 coincided with the collapse of the Soviet Union and a huge wave of privatization and liberalization. The end of the Cold War meant that power shifted further in the direction of the rich, liberal "first world" countries led by the United States. Indeed, the United States removed its crucial support of the racist South African government only because the collapse of Soviet socialism effectively ended the chance of a successful socialist transformation in South Africa. At an historical moment when state-owned industries in the former Soviet Union were being sold to a small number of extremely wealthy "oligarchs," South Africa's transformation was sure to involve more, rather than less, state control of economic production. The IMF and the United States crucially insisted that the new ANC government not only renege on its promises to take over key industries, but also reduce regulations and taxes to actually improve protections for both local and foreign capital.

The retired South African politician Ronnie Kasrils recently wrote the following summary of the ANC economic policies adopted following Mandela's election:

> All means to eradicate poverty, which was Mandela's and the ANC's sworn promise to the "poorest of the poor," were lost in the process [of transition to a post-apartheid government]. Nationalization of the mines and heights of the economy as envisaged by the Freedom Charter was abandoned. The ANC accepted responsibility for a vast apartheid-era debt, which should have been cancelled. A wealth tax on the super-rich to fund developmental projects was set aside, and domestic and international corporations, enriched by apartheid, were excused from any financial reparations. Extremely tight budgetary obligations were instituted that would tie the hands of any future governments; obligations to implement a free-trade policy and abolish all forms of tariff protection in keeping with neo-liberal free trade fundamentals were accepted. Big corporations were allowed to shift their main listings abroad. (Kasrils 2013: n.p.)

In the place of socialized mines and banks, what emerged in South Africa after 1994 was a new kind of welfare state, one that did indeed exhibit a tendency toward higher economic equality, but only insofar as it boosted the aggregate aid to the poor black population while lowering aggregate aid to the poor white population (Seekings and Nattrass 2008: 377).

The new welfare benefits introduced in South Africa during the 1990s include benefits for the elderly, disabled, and children among the black population. However, these new forms of aid very pointedly do not include benefits for unemployed people. Because unemployment in South Africa is found disproportionality within black communities, the result of this omission is that the needs of most poor black people are left unaddressed. The only way for most unemployed people to receive welfare benefits is as a member of a family that includes a child, an elderly person, or a disabled person.

68

The work of one ethnographer, Bernard Dubbeld, alerts us to the way that the jobless in South Africa remain not only outside the welfare state, but also outside of society in general. Dubbeld's fieldwork takes place in the rural village of Glendale, not far from the city of Durban. The local economy in Glendale has languished since the closure of a sugar mill there in 1997, and the residents of the town currently include a few retired workers from the sugar mill and fewer than 100 households of poor and unemployed people who moved there following the creation of a low-income housing settlement in 2002. Most people in Glendale are unemployed, and have little hope of finding employment by moving elsewhere. As the reader might expect, many people in Glendale attempt to escape poverty and unemployment by going into business for themselves—selling whatever inexpensive goods or needed services they can. Still, the possibilities for this sort of start-up entrepreneurship in Glendale are minimal. As one of Dubbeld's informants points out, "people don't have the means to buy much and lots of people are trying to sell something, and nobody can make anything here" (Dubbeld 2013a: 198).

Dubbeld suspects that around 70 per cent of households rely solely on government welfare grants to survive. While the state therefore provides minimal forms of housing, infrastructure, and the means of subsistence for most residents of Glendale, there is nevertheless a persistent feeling by many inhabitants that their village has been ignored and forgotten by those in power. Part of this is because much of the housing and infrastructure that has been provided by the state is either inadequate or in disrepair (Figure 6.1).

More broadly, however, it would seem that people in the village feel ignored or forgotten precisely because government benefits succeed in allowing them to survive but fail to encourage anything like a robust economy in or around the village. By and large, there is no functioning economic production nearby and no important economic ties to the outside world except those provided by welfare benefits themselves. Most people in Glendale very much desire a return to some kind of working prosperity, so that wages from work might again flow through the village economy.

Figure 6.1 Glendale housing.

In Dubbeld's own words, "almost everybody living in the village emphasizes some kind of absence of the state, arguing specifically that the democratic administration is 'invisible' and 'impersonal.'" Here is one example of this kind of claim:

A slightly older informant, 55-year-old Angelina, worked at the sugar mill and received one of the barrack houses when the mill closed in 1997. She does not receive a pension from that work, however, and looks after five of her grandchildren, relying on the Child Support Grant for income. She warns that while that grant is visibly helping people across the village, it is less clear "what people should eat if they have no child?"... She also tells me that "[former President] Thabo Mbeki never came to Glendale. [President] Zuma only stopped at Maphumulo, he did not come here. He should not rely on hearsay and talk about us in Glendale, as if he has seen the kind of life we are living."

The problem for Angelina is not only with the logic guiding the distribution of social assistance. Because she does not see those she considers her leaders, she believes the social circumstances she and those around her experience are invisible to government. She assumes a reciprocal mode of seeing in which her not seeing leaders of government is an expression of their not seeing her. Malusi, a seventy-year-old man who worked casually for many years in the sugar mill before it closed, also emphasizes the importance of visibility by arguing that "you can't be happy with something you don't see, and therefore we can't be happy with our councilor, our municipality and our government." (Dubbeld 2013b: 495)

In Dubbeld's analysis, what is crucial about the idiom of *seeing* and *being seen* is the way that it gestures toward the absence of a specifically *reciprocal* relationship between people. In order for a conversation to function, two people must be able to focus (visually or otherwise) on one another. By analogy, societies function when many people can "see" each other—that is, when they are able to understand and communicate together. Receiving government assistance means little in terms of respect, inclusion, and reciprocity.

Dubbeld hints at something else that is missing from village life—*value*: "Amid the palpable absence of waged work—but where waged work has remained the basis of value—the only site of hope is the government, and hence people want more government. Yet the state's incapacity to create waged work leaves it able only to maintain people and not to facilitate a transformed future" (2013b: 509). For the residents of Glendale, it is painfully clear that, as unemployed people, they remain outside of society. To return again briefly to the category of the citizen mentioned in the previous chapter, Dubbeld (2013b: 508) comes to the stark conclusion that "it is not the state that ensures citizenship ... but rather the sale and purchase of labor power." Without work, the residents of Glendale feel themselves not only left behind and isolated, but actually noncitizens of the South African nation.

To return to a theme from Chapter 3, what is at stake here is not only the movement of economic goods into and around Glendale; what is at stake is the morality of exchange. People in Glendale consume goods on a basis that renders them "invisible" and places their basic status as citizens in question. The welfare state secures a livelihood for these people, but it also cements their alienation from society at large. From an anthropological perspective, this alienation is the object of crucial concern when considering the welfare state.

The Welfare State and the "Perversity Thesis"

The flip side of the alienation felt by unemployed recipients of state-based welfare is the stigmatization of this sort of group in public discourse. For more than four decades, the sociologist Frances Fox Piven (1998: 21) has written about how public discussion concerning welfare tends to focus on "the perverse effects of cash assistance on the personal morality of recipients." That is to say, discussions about welfare almost inevitably devolve into discussions about the morality of the people who receive welfare, rather than the larger moral relationships entangled in the welfare state itself. Some good examples of this sort of discourse have been collected by the sociologists Margaret Somers and Fred Block. The following excerpt cataloged by Somers and Block is from the Domestic Policy Council, an office of the United States government that offers official policy advice to the US president: "The welfare system discourages work and self-reliance. The value of welfare's tax-free benefits often exceeds usable income from taxable work. While most Americans expect and want to work, welfare can seduce people into a life of dependency. Worst, the pattern and values of dependency can be transmitted from parent to child, who may come to see welfare as the social norm" (quoted in Somers and Block 2005: 234).

The language used here is at once highly moralistic and highly abstract. It is moralistic because it frames the receipt of welfare benefits as helping to create a category of abject personhood: the welfare recipient is different from most Americans because she or he (and it is most often women who are represented in this way) has been "seduced" into a state of "dependency." It is abstract because it frames this abject status as part of a systemic failure of political governance. Abject personhood, in this discourse, can be related to policy decisions rather than to the larger arrangement of social relation. Somers and Block refer here to the "perversity thesis"—that is, the notion that welfare systematically creates perverse incentives that undermine the sorts of work needed to sustain society as a whole.

The problem with the perversity thesis is that it fails to take account of what life is really like as a welfare recipient and instead substitutes judgments from a fully detached perspective. In many cases, the most obvious alternative to the reception of welfare benefits is low-wage work. As the sociologists and ethnographers Kathryn Edin and Laura Lein conclude about the United States, "single mothers chose the harsh world of welfare because that of low-wage work was even more grim" (quoted in Somers and Block 2005: 234). Making welfare recipients into abject persons necessarily entails the belief that low-wage work is a morally good thing. This is clear from the perspective of private employers and consumers, both of whom benefit from low-wage work and whose self-interest in this regard is seen as salutary. But implicit endorsements of low-wage work fail to capture how the self-interest of welfare recipients can be negated by taking it up. Potential low-wage workers are in a curious bind: either they can work in a way that might benefit themselves but will inevitably help their more well-off peers, or they can choose not to work and benefit only themselves. This is a moral dilemma only if one accepts the absurd notion of a duty to help the more well-off.

How are ethnographers to deal with the "perversity thesis" and the sorts of moral perspectives that it engenders? The anthropologists Sandra Morgen and Jeff Maskovsky (2003: 315) have suggested that ethnographic investigation of the welfare state focus on "exploring the multiple per-spectives of those differently situated within the welfare-state apparatus." This multi-perspectivalism is indeed crucial in my own experience. In my own ethnographic work on the sorts of language used in and around the German welfare state (McGill 2009), I have tried to follow Morgen and Maskovsky's advice, describing how people take up different sorts of conversational roles that reflect their involvement in the distribution and reception of welfare benefits. Political leaders and welfare-state profession-als (such as social workers) tend to represent themselves as disinterested participants in the institutional aspects of welfare provision. Welfare benefit recipients, however, do not generally have this luxury. Their perspective is taken seriously by others only when they position themselves as capable of commenting on the welfare state only from their own self-interested perspective. What emerges from this arrangement is a curious situation, in which people have the greater share of power when they are also capable of striking a disinterested pose. In Morgen and Maskovsky's terms, what we have is an arrangement of perspectives on the welfare state, some of which are privileged above others.

What an anthropological analysis of the welfare state suggests, therefore, is that this institution participates in the production of inequality insofar as it helps to maintain different situated subject positions. The welfare state is a force for economic equality insofar as it provides economic goods to the least well-off. But it is a force for inequality in moral status, insofar as the perspectives of welfare recipients are systematically discounted. The moralistic "perversity thesis" is notable for the way that it implies that there is a fixed agreement between people to work even when that work ben-efits others more than themselves. We should reject this kind of thinking about implicit "social contracts" in favor of an understanding of society as an interrelated network of individuals who help to generate one another's subject positions and points of view, each of which is of equal worth.

The Welfare State, Dignity, and Sharing

What the above analysis indicates is a need to describe the welfare state in terms of moral categories such as dignity and sharing. As we saw while discussing undocumented immigration in the previous chapter, the terms we use to analyze the welfare state make a great deal of difference to our understanding. For example, describing welfare benefits as "handouts" emphasizes the function of welfare benefits to distribute economic goods in a single direction, from the state to beneficiaries. By contrast, many welfare benefits can be described in more clinical terms as "social insurance"—a term used to imply that people pay taxes when they are working to fund the benefits they receive during retirement, disability, or periods of unemployment. Nevertheless, even the notion of social insurance draws attention to the fact that welfare benefits are directed stereotypically toward the misfortunate.

Over the past several decades, a group of political scientists have begun to accumulate some interesting findings in this vein. These scholars have begun with the simple and widely appreciated fact that many people living within liberal nation-states are reluctant to support the existence of welfare benefits (see Korpi and Palme 1998; Larsen 2008; Brooks and Manza 2008). In more specific terms, however, what these scholars have shown is that most opponents of the welfare state are specifically concerned about the existence of benefits targeted at the poorest members of society. Focusing on the United States, Christian Albrekt Larsen (2007: 165) has argued that most of the US public is willing to provide generous welfare benefits to society at large, but that they nevertheless harbor a "specific antiegalitarian attitude toward the bottom."[1] That is to say, most people in the United States are willing to share the fruits of their labors with one another, but most of them also do not want to share their income with the poorest members of society. Because benefits to the poorest members of society are actually the most important for bare survival, the result is a vicious circle. Political opponents who object to redistribution to the poorest members of society may succeed in reducing overall expenditures, but not in completely eliminating the lowest levels of the social safety net. The result is a welfare state that is increasingly identified with only the poorest members of society, which in turn feeds suspicion and distrust of welfare beneficiaries. Speaking in a different context, the anthropologists Rob Higham and Alpa Shah (2013: 82) have referred to the result of this kind of dynamic as a weakened "state of the poor."

Since the welfare state actually becomes weaker the more it focuses on providing aid to people in their moment of greatest need, it is no surprise that countries with the most robust welfare states focus *both* on aid to genuinely needy people *and* on the widespread distribution of services within the population at large. A good example of this is Denmark, the country that I mentioned in Chapter 3 as the most egalitarian in the world according to measurements of the Gini coefficient. The Danish government provides free universal health care and free education through the university level, including an allowance for the living expenses of college students. Disability and unemployment benefits are relatively high, and all parents receive a special cash benefit for each child in their household. According to one international organization, nearly a third of the spending in the Danish economy goes toward this type of social

---

1 For a discussion of the "envy up, scorn down" dynamic, which particularly strongly isolates the least well-off as objects of scorn, see Fiske (2011).

expenditure.[2] Funding a social state of this size is costly, and income taxes for the most wealthy can be as high as 60 per cent. Of course, the welfare state in Denmark is far from a source of jubilation, and it does draw its share of detractors (see Daley 2013). Policy makers in Denmark have reduced the levels of some of the lowest-level unemployment benefits over the course of the last decade. However, they have done little to actually reduce the overall level of welfare spending. By focusing on the provision of basic services for society at large, rather than simply on the amelioration of poverty, Denmark remains the world's most egalitarian country.

Denmark is also among the wealthiest countries in the world. Unsurprisingly, then, there are many countries where the provision of widespread basic human services simply does not come into question. Still, the basic principle remains that the welfare state is strongest when it is consistent with the dignity of the people who receive benefits. A good example of what I mean by this involves Brazil, where the *Bolsa Família* program initiated in 2003 has made great strides in reducing extreme poverty. *Bolsa Família* provides cash benefits to poor families, some of which are given on an unconditional basis and some of which require that any children in a family receiving the grant attend school and receive vaccinations. One World Bank economist (Lindert 2005) has estimated that *Bolsa Família* costs only about a half of 1 per cent of Brazil's gross national product, and yet could remove as many as 40 million people from extreme poverty. Related programs throughout Latin America and the Caribbean show similar promise.

While these sorts of reductions in poverty are extremely important, it is also crucial to remember that they may not result in equally sizable reductions in strictly economic inequality. A child receiving benefits under Brazil's *Bolsa Família* program may be living on $2 per day, rather than $1 per day. This change in income may substantially change that child's access to clean water and regular meals—a good that cannot be underestimated. Still, *Bolsa Família* benefits do little to change that child's overall position in society. And while the aggregated effects of *Bolsa Família* may help to create moderate reductions in Brazil's rates of economic inequality, the fact of the matter is that Brazil remains an extremely unequal country even after these effects have been accounted for. According to World Bank statistics, the top 10 per cent of Brazilians earned 43 per cent of the country's income in 2009, while the bottom 10 per cent earned less than 1 per cent of the country's income.[3] While the program may make substantial changes in the actual livelihoods of the poorest residents of Brazil, there is little reason

---

2 OECD data, Social Expenditure Database (SOCX). Available at http://www.oecd.org/social/expenditure.htm.

3 World Bank data (PovcalNet). Available at http://iresearch.worldbank.org/PovcalNet/index.htm?3.

to think that *Bolsa Família* will succeed in making anything more than minor changes to the basic distribution of income.[4]

Of course, measurements of income are not the only way to consider economic inequality. Beginning in 1990, the economist and moral philosopher Amartya Sen collaborated with the United Nations Development Programme to publish an annual index of "human development" across countries. This index is based on the notion that the most important form of equality involves the equal use of basic "human capabilities" (see Sen 1993). Rather than measuring income or wealth, the human development index measures a composite of life expectancy, education and literacy, and standard of living. While a program such as *Bolsa Família* might do little to reduce income or wealth inequality, it could do much to reduce inequality in human development. In the transnational perspective typically adopted by the United Nations, these sorts of guaranteed-income welfare programs have the potential to substantially reduce human development inequality across countries.

In more political terms, what seems most interesting about programs such as *Bolsa Família* is that they have something to do with dignity. Rather than proposing that aid should go only to a special category of the deserving poor (such as the disabled, children, or even unemployed people), programs such as these affirm that basic aid should be available to everyone who lives in extreme poverty. The title of a recent book—*Just Give Money to the Poor: The Development Revolution from the Global South* (Hanlon, Barrientos, and Hulme 2010)—starkly illustrates the emergence of a new philosophy of direct and unconditional welfare transfers to those in extreme poverty.

In spite of this "development revolution," the anthropologist Gregory Duff Morton has described the insecurity that remains for families who receive *Bolsa Família*. In May 2013, nearly a million people took to the streets following rumors of the program's disappearance. While these rumors proved to be unfounded, what Morton discovered was a widespread sentiment that "*Bolsa Família* is not something reliable. You can't count on this money," and that "*Bolsa Família* is not a sure thing that—today you've got it, tomorrow—you don't know any more if you have it" (quoted in Morton 2014: 927). The substantial change that the program had made in the lives of recipients could not be counted upon against the background of shifting governmental policies and perennially insecure political rights (see previous chapter). Even local administrators of the program remain wary, arguing that "it's a program that had a beginning and that can have an end ... the families have to prepare to disconnect themselves from it"

---

4 Indeed, there are convincing arguments that many Latin American nations have only recently begun to effect an overall redistribution of wealth to the poor through government programs. State programs in Latin America frequently still function as the actions of a "reverse Robin Hood," who funnels money from the poor to the more well-off (mostly in the form of state pensions). See Lindert, Skoufias, and Shapiro (2006).

(quoted in Morton 2014: 931). Morton (931) argues that *Bolsa Família* remains an "unstable gift" that gives proof of citizens' "inability to influence the decisions that most affect [their lives]." In the words of the ethnographers Talita Jabs Eger and Arlei Sander Damo (2014), the benefits provided by *Bolsa Família* remain a "special kind of money," not completely commensurate with other sources of income.

Morton points out that the panicked benefit recipients who took to the streets following rumors of the program's demise did not have a clearly formulated political position. Rather, they gathered as a collective expression of their own insecurity as people who are outsiders to both the political and the economic system. One important conclusion to make—and since it ventures somewhat outside of the direct ethnographic evidence offered by Morton, it is perhaps better to call it a hypothesis—is that the beneficiaries of programs like *Bolsa Família* will be secure only once they are able to combine the sorts of political equality at stake in the previous chapter with the kinds of economic equality at issue here. While *Bolsa Família* recipients may be able to maintain their basic dignity, and are not necessarily subject to the "perversity thesis" described by Somers and Block (2005), they remain in an unstable position with regards to their ability to depend on the program's benefits. Increasing their political power as "insurgent citizens" would serve to alter this predicament and further enhance their dignity in the nation at large.

Conclusion

Because this chapter and the last are so closely interrelated, it is worth offering some conclusions that bring them together. The liberal regimes that are currently hegemonic in the world today are generally aligned with both political equality and economic inequality. This would seem to present us with the illusion that political equality, such as the end of apartheid in South Africa, has been bought at the price of ongoing economic inequality, such as that which is only barely ameliorated by the South African welfare state. It might also present us with the tempting notion that greater economic equality could be won by surrendering to greater political inequality. What is at stake here, however, is not a trade-off between different forms of inequality, but rather the complex intersection of these different forms (see Chapter 3). Inequality must be addressed as a singular problem, rather than as an act of balancing the guarantee of rights, the distribution of income, the achievement of human capabilities, and so on. This means that no single form of equality is adequate on its own and, more to the point, that the liberal primacy of equal rights over material equality should not be treated as an end point for human society. The quest for greater, more complete forms of equality goes on—both within and among nation-states.

CHAPTER 7

RESISTANCE AND SOCIAL ORGANIZATION
IN AN UNEQUAL WORLD

In the first chapter, I described Geertz's approach to anthropology as involving "thinking as a moral act." It is important to point out, however, that inequality is not merely something to contemplate. Inequality is an experience that, on at least some occasions, motivates people to action. In this chapter, I am therefore concerned with the particular relationship between inequality and organized social action. To elucidate this concern, I sketch three different ethnographic cases in China, Argentina, and Israel.

Life in the Global Factory

A good place to start any discussion of organized attempts to combat social inequality is with those particular forms of inequality that have emerged during the course of industrial growth in China. The economist Branko Milanovic has pointed out that there have been two groups of "winners" from the past 20 years of globalization. The first group is the hyperelite—that is, those at the very top of the global income scale. During the period in question, this group has seen income growth of 60 per cent. Of course, this growth represents a rather large amount of money for each person involved, since the people representing this group were already immensely wealthy to begin with. However, a much poorer group of people has matched the top of the global income scale strictly in terms of percentile income *growth* (Figure 7.1). I am referring to the "global middle class," whose income gains have largely come through Chinese industrialization. While many people scattered around the world can be associated with this income group, it is overwhelmingly industrial workers

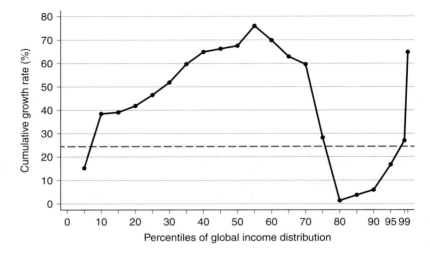

Figure 7.1 Growth in income, distributed by income groups.

Visible on the far right of the graph is the income growth experienced by the wealthiest global inhabitants. The much wider peak of income growth in the center of the graph is largely attributable to industrialization in China.

Source: Lakner and Milanovic 2013.

in China who have experienced a substantial change in their livelihood during the past 20 years.

As I have already hinted, information about income growth must be kept in perspective with respect to the already existing distribution of global income. Drastic inequalities still exist between those at the middle of the income distribution (whose income is less than $10 a day) and those situated further up. Moreover, it is not merely income that differentiates these groups. Specifically with reference to China, the income gains made through rapid industrialization have occurred only at the price of nearly constant and extremely demanding work. Life in the global factory is bleak, with shifts lasting as long as 12 hours six or seven days a week, with highly unsafe or unhealthy working conditions, and with living conditions limited to the extremely spartan confines of factory-owned dormitories. The demand for (and exploitation of) female labor has been particularly strong, as young rural women are often seen as "docile, cheap and young" by potential employers (Xin 2008: 516).

Most factory workers in China are rural-to-urban migrants, and the Chinese government's system of residency permits (*hukou*) means that these migrants are in a particularly vulnerable position. Rural villagers who move to big cities to work in factories generally do not have an unlimited right to live in those cities. This means that they are very often at the mercy of their employers, since being out of a job even temporarily means being homeless and subject to expulsion back to a rural village. Rural-to-urban migrants are also largely without political power. In the words of one Chinese dissident, "Vulnerable groups [of migrant workers] lack the right to speak, to organize and to exercise oversight of government" (Xingdou 2009). Without the basic ability to legalize their residency, labor migrants are all but completely powerless against both factory owners and government officials.

In 1949, the Chinese Communist Party came to power in China after a long civil war. Led by Mao Zedong, the Communist Party enforced new forms of economic equality by stripping landlords and rich peasants of their property. Until 1978, China would be one of the most economically egalitarian countries in the world—largely because the country was made up overwhelmingly of poor rural peasants (see Riskin, Zhao, and Li 2001). The small working class that began to emerge around government-owned factories in northeastern China had significant advantages over village peasants, particularly in terms of lifetime job protection. As the sociologists Ching Kwan Lee and Mark Selden (2008) have argued, however, the most important class divisions in pre-1978 China were not between workers and peasants, but actually between socialist state officials and the ordinary working people living in villages and cities alike. The authoritarian policies of the Communist Party included the disastrous Great Leap Forward, which was intended to build industry and create an egalitarian and collectivist social structure beginning at the village level but instead largely resulted in haphazard, state-led production. In spite of these failures, the Communist Party managed to stay in power, leaving privileged state officials in a position of unique power. It was against the background of the division between these privileged state officials and ordinary citizens that the policy of "opening up" to global forms of private capital began in the 1980s. The establishment of privately owned factories and the collapse of rural land prices have encouraged members of the large peasant population to migrate to cities as factory workers and temporary residents. In spite of this surge of private capitalist investment and migrant proletarianization, China officially remains a communist country. This arrangement has allowed state bureaucrats to "commodify" their official positions through a massive network of insider deals with private capitalists.

Today, economic inequality in China is growing rapidly even as industrialization allows for the country as a whole to move toward a middle-income status. This new inequality is characterized by what Lee and Selden (2008: 31) describe as "an alliance of officials and private capital," which together have succeeded in exploiting very large numbers of rural-to-urban migrants.

And while government officials and private capitalists have benefited most from this arrangement, it is important to point out that the exploitation of rural-to-urban migrants is largely supported by urban Chinese of every social class. Rural-to-urban migrants—the engine of economic growth—are frequently looked down on as status inferiors by those who have been officially granted urban status.

Given this historical backdrop, what kind of organized attempts might be undertaken by rural-to-urban migrant factory workers? In her ethnographic work, Lee (2006) has described how disaffected factory workers have at best succeeded in mounting instances of "cellular resistance"—that is, sporadic and isolated protests against the actions of a particular set of factory bosses. Since protesting workers at an individual factory can be easily replaced, the most effective forms of labor protest would require organization across many factories. Because workers are not usually able to link their struggles across factory sites, they are able to receive only small concessions while risking violence and imprisonment on an arbitrary basis. As the ethnographer and labor studies scholar Eli Friedman (2014) has shown, moreover, the state effectively co-opts this form of organization. Ostensibly dedicated to shared ownership and prosperity based on the solidarity of the working class, the state presumes to speak for workers' interests in a universal way. Lee further describes how workers feel discouraged from speaking about their interests as a class (*jieji*), since that term is generally associated with the ruling Communist Party. Instead, they are likely to refer to "workers' personal interests" (*gongren de chexinliyi*) in the wealth produced in a single factory.

It seems important, in this regard, that even when workers are organizing collectively to receive better wages and working conditions, they feel compelled to take up a discourse concerned with their individual economic interests. Lee (2006: 31) concludes that "if class subjectivity has any empowering consequence for protesting workers, it resides in the specific notion of collective ownership of any enterprise," but that unemployment can undermine these claims because it breaks the bonds between a particular worker and the factory in which she or he works. Workers are compelled to address their individual interests but remain largely powerless without the ability to organize these individual interests across factories.

The individualization of Chinese factory workers actually begins long before protest is even a possibility. The anthropologist Yan Hairong (2003: 494) has emphasized how rural-to-urban migrant workers in China are individualized through a discourse centered on the notion of *suzhi*, a word which can be translated as "quality" and can refer, more specifically, to notions such as "civility, self-discipline and modernity." The anthropologist Andrew Kipnis (2006: 297) has similarly emphasized how *suzhi* "marks the hierarchical and moral distinction between the high and the low."

The Chinese government has articulated the specific goal of developing and inculcating *suzhi* among migrant workers as part of a self-conscious attempt to develop the national economy through the development of individualized forms of refinement and self-discipline. "Improving the suzhi of China's massive population has become vitally important in the planning of governing elites for China to become a competitive player in the field of global capital" (Hairong 2003: 494). Hairong points out, however, that this discourse is also adopted by educators, labor recruiters working in rural villages, and workers themselves. Talk about *suzhi* functions to put an emphasis on the actions of individual workers, rather than on collec-   **81** tive concerns. In local villages, labor recruiters hold up young women who have returned from working as domestic servants in cities as paragons of modernity and sophistication, encouraging other village women to emulate their behavior in a way that makes them conveniently exploitable. For this sort of uneducated and poor village woman, a strictly individual model of personal development is held up as "her salvation" (Hairong 2003: 506).

Kipnis has emphasized how inequality, competition, and the notion of *suzhi* feed on one another. As inequality in China increases, individual people are more anxious about their ability to compete with others, which in turn encourages them to think more explicitly in terms of individual *suzhi*. "As inequality becomes more visible, the anxiety generated by the possibility of falling behind increases competition to attain the trappings of suzhi" (Kipnis 2006: 310). This individualistic notion, however, also provides an important alibi for inequality, since it is presumably those with more *suzhi* who are inherently deserving of greater wealth and status. This reinforcing cycle constitutes a good example of what I referred to in Chapter 4 as involving the production of inequality.

Of course, the organization of factory workers in China has important economic constraints that go along with the discursive ones described above. By now, it is a well-known axiom of globalization that successful attempts to increase wages threaten the "offshoring" of manufacturing jobs to new locations. Since the early 2010s, there have been clear signs that rising wages in China are beginning to encourage investors to build factories in other countries, especially nearby Asian countries such as Vietnam. Nevertheless, the size of the billion-person Chinese labor market and the massive success of Chinese industrialization strongly suggest that struggles by Chinese workers for better pay and working conditions are a potential watershed in global labor organization. Ethnographers who are well informed about the global economic context have every reason to look closely at the progress of labor organization in China.

In a very interesting turn of events, the advent of the Internet means that scholars studying labor unrest in China have the opportunity to collaborate with the workers they hope to study. An excellent example of this are the Friends of Gongchao, a group that currently operates the website gongchao.org and has collaborated with scholars based out of Europe, North America, and China to better document factory life and workplace organization. The work of this collective ranges from blog posts up to print books edited by established anthropologists, sociologists, and others. The Friends of Gongchao (*gongchao* means "strike" or "workers' movement") have also helped to forge ties with labor activists in other countries, such as the workers at an electronics factory in Wrocław, Poland, owned by Chung Hong Electronics, a Taiwanese corporation that also has an extensive factory presence in mainland China (Figure 7.2).

82

From an ethnographic perspective, what is interesting about the work of the Friends of Gongchao is the way that their work publicly presents a persona for factory workers that is different from one based on the image of the *suzhi*-seeking striver. The factory worker represented on the group's websites and its publications is an avid protester, resister, and networker. Pictures, text, and video on gongchao.org, for example, validate the struggle against factory owners as a source of identity.

Horizontalidad

Many readers of this book will be familiar with the Occupy movement, which began in the fall of 2011 with a protest encampment in downtown Manhattan known as Occupy Wall Street. The concern at the center of this protest was growing income inequality in the United States, especially as effected by the profits of large financial corporations. Inspired by the initial gathering in New York, similar protests against economic inequality occurred across the North American continent, from Portland and Sacramento to Montreal and Washington, DC. Similar protests were also organized in many cities around the world, and in many cases, the Occupy protest movement merged with existing local protest movements. Protests in Spain beginning several months before Occupy Wall Street were particularly notable, as were later protests in Greece and Turkey. Taking note of these various movements, the activists and authors Marina Sitrin and Dario Azzellini (2014: 5) have characterized the global situation today as involving a "growing global movement of refusal."

In addition to scholarship surveying the global protest scene, Sitrin has also produced a series of more detailed dossiers on the emergence of a new collectivist movement in Argentina associated with the notion of *horizontalidad* ("horizontalism"). This movement was catalyzed by the economic and financial crisis of 1998–2001, which reached its climax when the government froze bank accounts to avoid mass withdrawals of savings and the collapse of banks. In December 2001, millions of Argentines took to the streets to protest this action, quickly toppling the national government. Once a new government was installed, political leaders called for a default

Figure 7.2 Strikers at a factory near Wrocław, Poland
Source: http://www.gongchao.org/en/texts/2013/strike-in-chinese-company-in-polish-sez.

on Argentine public debt and, eventually, the devaluation of the Argentine currency as a means to stem the crisis. These measures allowed the Argentine economy to recover, but in the meantime, millions of jobs had been lost, and millions of middle-class people had been thrown into poverty. In the wake of this lasting economic trauma, it was unemployed middle-class people who would largely lead the movement to create the more "horizontal" social structures documented by Sitrin.

A prominent example of these structures involves the recuperation of shuttered factories by unemployed workers. The documentary film *The Take* (2004) shows how workers in one automobile parts factory broke in, refurbished machines, acquired new customers, and began to issue their own products. Under the motto "Occupy, resist, produce," these workers managed to create their own business within which all workers are paid the same wage and decisions are made democratically within a worker assembly. Sitrin and Azzellini (2014: 185) have also described how large numbers of Argentine people have organized neighborhood assemblies to support community life and replace disappearing social services. The work of the assemblies is described as follows: "In each neighborhood the assemblies worked, and many continue to work, on a variety of projects, including helping to facilitate barter networks, creating popular kitchens, providing alternate medicine, planting organic gardens, and sometimes taking over buildings—including the highly symbolic creation of community centers in the shells of abandoned banks. These occupied spaces house kitchens, small print shops, day-care areas, after-school help for children, libraries, micro-enterprises, and free internet access and computer usage; one even has a small movie theater."

Like the occupied factories, these assemblies are the result of *autogestión*, or local self-management. Participants eschew hierarchies and formal structures in favor of *horizontalidad* and consensus-building. Sitrin has emphasized that these sorts of organizations can be fragile and short-lived, especially when they enter into conflict with state power.

More tellingly, however, Sitrin has also emphasized how these types of horizontal movements require a change in the people who are participating:

> If the assemblies disappeared, it wouldn't be so terrible. I say this because there's something happening in people right now—a real change. And this is really important for building whatever kind of future—it doesn't matter what kind exactly. I think the most important thing, with respect to the neighborhood assemblies, is that they've created a profound change in people's subjectivity. People who believed they were never going to do anything again, all of a sudden did. This is especially important considering our society, which teaches us that nothing done collectively matters, and that the only important thing is the individual. Just the fact that people have started to realize they can do things collectively is really important. (Sitrin 2006: 216)

Elsewhere, Sitrin has emphasized these changes as involving a new kind of attitude—one that prizes the ability of people to be protagonists in their own lives above the ability of the nation as a whole to produce value on economic investments. She provides the following quotation from an informant named Martin:

> I believe that there's more creative protagonism when there isn't so much focus on the individual. I say this, in part, because the person I am today isn't who I used to be. I'm still getting to know myself, and undergoing an existential transformation that's teaching me a different way of being in the world. I changed my relationship with the world, and because I'm basically in another world, I live differently, I see differently, and I can understand society differently. This is partly because I've had the experience of trying to live in the world in another way for a year and five months—the time since the rebellion and emergence of the neighborhood assemblies and other movements. (Sitrin 2006: 218)

This shift in consciousness is particularly interesting when we consider it in the light of some of the insights from the previous section. While *suzhi* can be described as a cultural category caught up with both individualization and inequality, *horizontalidad* and *autogestión* can be described as cultural categories that are caught up with both collectivization and equality.

Because I have created a comparison between China and Argentina, it is important to point out the major differences between these two countries. In spite of the major economic downturn in 1998, Argentina has long been a middle-income country—indeed, one of the richest countries in Latin America. Middle-class people who have lost good-paying jobs through a shared economic crisis have been at the core of new horizontal movements. By contrast, China has only recently transitioned from a largely rural economy to one that includes a major concentration of industrial production. The power of a category such as *suzhi* can be understood only in the context of huge numbers of people seeking entrance into the global middle class for the first time. Similarly, the power of concepts such as *horizontalidad* and *autogestión* would seem to be limited in some ways by their association with a previously established middle class. As both Sitrin and *The Take* make clear, it is not at all a given that groups of extremely poor people would have the financial wherewithal, the technical skills, or the social status to make a success of the kind of collectivization that has occurred, at least sporadically, in Argentina.

Inequality, Competition, and Middle-Class Ownership

An important conclusion to draw from the examples of *horizontalidad* provided by Sitrin is that the power of a protest movement depends on how the people who take part in that movement are situated in society.

I'd like to begin the final section of this chapter by looking in on some protests of a strikingly different character than the wildcat strikes of Chinese factory workers and the Occupy-style protests that occurred around the world several years ago.

During the summer of 2011, a series of protests erupted in the Israeli city of Tel Aviv. The anthropologist Hadas Weiss (2014: 128) sets the scene for these protests in the following way: "The uprising billed itself as targeting the high cost of living in general, but its casus belli was housing, as evidenced by the multiple tent encampments that sprang up overnight. In less than a decade, housing prices in Israel have practically doubled with rents becoming prohibitive and homeownership slipping ever further out of reach."

While it is customary for ethnographers to witness and describe protest movements, and even to link those protest movements to a variety of social categories, Weiss sets herself the more unusual task of understanding the situated economic thinking of these "middle-class protests." These protesters are clearly concerned about the social justice necessary to maintain reasonable housing costs, but their lives outside of their protest activity do not often reflect these imperatives.

Weiss frames the thinking of her middle-class ethnographic informants in terms of a series of paradoxes—most crucially, she describes how middle-class people who already own a home benefit from rising real estate prices, yet remain deeply anxious about the real estate market that their children will encounter. Most middle-class Israelis depend on their parents to help them afford the down payment for a new home, and so rising real estate costs are a large source of stress even for those who have already entered the real estate market decades before. In addition, rental housing is often insecure and inadequate, requiring renters to relocate to a new apartment every few years as landlords raise rents, sell their holdings, or refurbish property.

The result is a deep vein of public support for affordable housing, albeit one that is rarely expressed in the collective form achieved in the summer of 2011. There are some very structural reasons why this occurs. In Weiss's words, the protest movement in favor of more widely affordable housing remains mired in the competing interests of intergenerational households:

> While social injustice incites public outrage, the pressures of
> reproducing a stable domestic sphere discourage protesters from
> prioritizing their common cause. To secure their own futures they
> must relate to one another as competing investors and consider rent
> paid to others as money "thrown away." In turn, they ally themselves
> with banks that leverage their investments, as well as with state

institutions that protect the value of these investments. . . . Credit dissolves political agency, first by pitting one struggling household against the other, and second, by linking financially-leveraged growth to public interest, even when such leveraging systemically undermines common welfare and security. (Weiss 2014: 144–45)

What Weiss sketches out here is a deep contradiction centered on the middle-class identities of Israeli protestors, who are torn by their shared demands for a more reasonable cost of living and their competition with one another to access mortgage-financed real estate. Weiss suggests that a less "paradoxical" arrangement would involve housing policies that encourage affordable and stable rental housing but that such a solution is not possible precisely because of the tendency of middle-class people to prioritize home ownership.

In the years to come, the immediate contradictions involved in this situation may be altered by a sudden drop in housing prices. However, even economic experts have agreed that an Israeli housing market bubble can sustain itself as long as middle-class consumers in the housing market maintain their belief that housing should be and should remain expensive (see Shiller 2014). On a deeper level, however, what Weiss points to is the fact that the large-scale workings of the credit market make it difficult for people to see one another as participating in shared solutions to, for example, the provision of housing on a widespread basis. At best, the result of this is a boom-and-bust real estate market that arbitrarily benefits some and arbitrarily harms others. At worst, it makes for a sustained disorganization among shared economic interests, such that meaningful solutions to shared problems remain perpetually out of reach.

The results of this for the growth of inequality also seem clear— competition between individuals both encourages and justifies forms of inequality that do not necessarily have anything to do with safeguarding economic well-being. If Weiss's work is any indication of the future, anthropologists will increasingly be witness to the disarrangements of markets—that is, the ways in which markets can be patently insufficient for satisfying shared desires for material goods. The need of middle-class actors to get ahead of the market means that they are perpetually attempting to get ahead of one another, rather than focusing on collective aspects of their lives. Indeed, it would seem that this can even occur alongside widespread and dramatic public protests in favor of greater social justice.

CHAPTER 8

SITUATED SUBJECTS IN AN UNEQUAL WORLD

In the previous chapter, I discussed various possibilities and limitations for the overt organization of people against economic inequality; however, people do not always deal with inequality in an overt way. Anthropologists are frequently concerned with *situated subjectivity* as a key aspect of ordinary culture, and in this chapter I describe some of the ways that minds and bodies alike are formed in relation to inequality. To put the point briefly, people are made through their ordinary interactions with one another, and when these interactions involve forms of inequality, people are bound to be formed, at least in part, based on their experience of inequality. What unfolds from this line of thinking is a series of interpretations of certain specific patterns of interaction as highly situated—and therefore highly implicit—attempts to deal with inequality.

Capital and *Confianza*: A Tale of Two Schools

If we are looking for places in which people are made, there is no better place to start than with schools. As social sciences of various disciplines have long noted, schools help to reproduce society by shaping young people. In the words of the anthropologists Dorothy C. Holland and Margaret A. Eisenhart (1990: 28), "what is learned [in schools] undergirds the structure of power and privilege in society." In the United States, it is the inequality between schools (and not simply within them) that most clearly plays a role in the creation of these sorts of structures. To begin with, US public school districts are largely funded by local communities, which means that the poorest communities have much fewer resources to educate students than do the wealthiest communities. One recent study has documented a range of annual expenditures per high school student from a low of around $4,000 to a high of around $15,000 (Biddle and Berliner 2003: 2–3).

Two schools that have been recent objects of ethnographic analysis— Wilton Burnham High School in suburban Ohio and El Pueblo High School in southern California—provide ready representatives of the two ends of this spectrum. Wilton Burnham is located in an affluent community; the school has abundant resources, a well-paid and highly motivated staff, a broad curriculum, and a substantial "co-curriculum" of artistic and athletic activities. Counselors work closely with students to help define career goals and steer students toward college. By contrast, El Pueblo High School is a place beset with problems. Teachers are demoralized and frequently fail to engage students in the most basic ways. Counselors are completely overburdened and are likely to see students only in large groups. The curriculum is limited, and the facilities have been described as "squalid" by Julio Cammarota, whose ethnography I discuss below.

In Peter Demerath's book (2009: 85) about Wilton Burnham, we find the claim that Burnham students are in possession of a certain quantity of "psychological capital," which has allowed them to develop "a whole suite of identity characteristics that are geared towards success—and control." Students at this school "have a sense that they are special, that their opinions matter," but also that "adults should, as a matter of routine, adjust situations to meet children's wishes" (43). Quoting from the sociologist David Riesman, Demerath explains how the schooling of upper-middle-class Americans encourages the habit of "manipulating others and being oneself manipulated" (5). The carefully calibrated "business culture" of personal advancement at Wilton Burnham gives students the power to demand engagement from their teachers (and sometimes simply to demand a higher grade than they have earned).

This same culture also creates a gnawing anxiety among students about their ability to maintain academic and extracurricular standards while preparing for a remorselessly competitive labor market. Demerath shows how students at the school spend long periods isolated from their peers and families, a burden that magnifies the constant pressure they feel from parents and teachers. The use of antidepressants and the drug Adderall (prescribed for ADHD, but also sold covertly as a study aid) are common, as are reports of children with "school phobia" (i.e., anxiety triggered merely by presence on school grounds) and anxiety attacks on campus. Responding to these issues, school administrators devised a "Stress Hurts" campaign, encouraging students to speak out about the anxiety they feel in everyday life. As the notion of "psychological capital" already suggests, however, the bright side of life at Wilton Burnham has more to do with enjoyment of life in the future than in the present. A competitive college application process and high costs of tuition mean that the best sorts of career preparation are most readily available to those who both work hard and have access to an excellent high school. Most of the students Demerath encounters earnestly believe in hard work and determination as a way to live a good life and take their achievements to heart as a form of validation regarding their pursuit of that life.

The future, both promising and distressing, is at the center of daily concerns at Wilton Burnham. This is not the case, however, at El Pueblo High School. Most students at El Pueblo come from poor families, and their parents typically work in low-wage service jobs. In Cammarota's telling, most students at El Pueblo are hardworking. In this case, however, working hard means balancing schoolwork with long hours at their own low-wage jobs. While their parents help to provide for students' daily needs, the students themselves must also help support their families by making financial contributions toward rent and living expenses. Cammarota describes how this economic cooperation within families (and especially the sharing of resources between parents and children) leads to a keen sense of what it means to be interdependent with other people, and indeed to establish meaningfully reciprocal relations with them. Very often, this interdependence is conceived of as "the delight of helping loved ones instead of as the pressure of family obligation" (Cammarota 2008: 54).

Helping support one's family through low-wage work obviously interferes with academic achievement insofar as wage work takes substantial time and energy. However, these responsibilities also undercut students' relationships with their overburdened and frequently demoralized teachers: "Evidence from young people's statements suggest that teachers and school personnel pay attention only to students who obviously demonstrate exceptional ability and overlook those seemingly unable to succeed. . . . Teachers and school personnel seem to believe that their job is to identify and educate those who show them first that they can succeed, while presupposing the failure of those not immediately revealing their potential" (Cammarota 2008: 129). In more blunt terms, "the normal experience in the El Pueblo school system … is widespread uncaring" (117). Most teachers simply do not see a future for their students beyond low-wage work, and so have little personal motivation to help improve those students' lives.

In an interesting contrast to the notion of "psychological capital," students at El Pueblo are described by Cammarota (2008: 162) as having a strong sense of *confianza*—a Spanish word glossed as "a kind of trust deeply connected with reciprocity and respect." Stress is more immediate for these students, as a result of their need to help their families and themselves maintain a livelihood at the bottom of the labor market. In Cammarota's account, most El Pueblo students have the day-to-day survival of their families, and not their own individual achievement, at the center of their minds. It is therefore unsurprising that they gain little from thinking of academic achievement as the reward for a strictly individual dedication of time and effort over the long term. It is not that they do not wish to attain an individualistic form of "psychological capital"; it is just that doing so is not as important as navigating the present defined by interdependence and reciprocity with their families.

By now, the irony of this arrangement should be clear. The students who are most likely to succeed are those who see both themselves and others as objects to exploit, while the students who are less likely to succeed are those who value relationships of trust and interdependence. Schools socialize students to these roles, which become crucial in the reproduction of social differences after graduation. High incomes and high levels of educational attainment become a way to valorize the individual and support what Cammarota calls the "ethos of individualism" dominant in society at large. At the same time, low-wage work is most likely to be seen as a means to help immediate family members, leaving the workers in these roles in a highly caring, yet clearly diminished, social position.

The Witchcraft of Modernity

Anthropologists have applied the concepts of *witchcraft* and *sorcery* to cultural groups around the world. However, these terms were originally borrowed from European contexts. The results are several. First, there are sometimes terminological difficulties involved in the use of these concepts. The resulting issues, one example of which is discussed below, can be difficult but not entirely impossible to untangle. Second, there is often confusion surrounding the relevance of these concepts to the modern world. Because witchcraft and sorcery beliefs are associated with the European past, there is a tendency to see similar sorts of beliefs as outdated or archaic. In a classical description by E.E. Evans-Pritchard, witchcraft beliefs among Azande people in central Africa are explicitly contrasted with the sorts of beliefs held by "educated Europeans" such as himself. Creating a clear dividing line between belief in witchcraft and a modern scientific worldview has generally allowed ethnographers to distinguish their own world from that of their research subjects.

In recent years, however, a series of anthropologists have sought to upset such divisions. Questioning the binary opposition between tradition and modernity, Jean and John L. Comaroff (1993: xviii) have suggested that witchcraft can be seen as a "situated moral discourse" that addresses all manner of typically modern experiences. Comaroff and Comaroff suggest that the forms of power that are most familiar in modern life—the bureaucratic wrangling of state officials, the relentless exploitation of workers by the owners of farms and businesses, and so on—are just as much in need of a cosmic explanation as are the sorts of events of illness and death first described by Evans-Pritchard in his Azande village ethnography. When it is applied to the vagaries of existence under capitalist economies and centralized states, witchcraft discourse can and does offer a compelling account of certain thoroughly modern experiences. Unlike Evans-Pritchard, Comaroff and Comaroff (1993: xi) characterize modern minds as inevitably beset by both material *and* spiritual concerns, arguing that modernity itself has always been "diverse and dynamic, multiple and multidirectional." There is a sense from Comaroff and Comaroff's argument that because the modern world is heterogeneous and incompletely realized, witchcraft discourse cannot help but address modern experience.

There have been several important ethnographic studies of witchcraft that have attempted to substantiate theoretical views similar to those suggested by Comaroff and Comaroff. The most thorough treatment, however, can be found in the work of Peter Geschiere. In his book *The Modernity of Witchcraft: Politics and Occult in Postcolonial Africa*, Geschiere's particular concern is with the category of the *djambe* among the Maka of eastern Cameroon, which he describes in the following way:

> The *djambe* is a force—or even a being—that lives in the belly of a person. It permits its proprietor to transform himself or herself into a spirit or an animal and to do all sorts of other exceptional things. This force can be used to kill and, according to my spokesmen, often is. One could therefore translate *djambe* as "witchcraft." But the same *djambe* ... can also be used in a more positive sense: for instance, to heal or to affirm one's prestige. Sometimes the term is used in such a general sense—for instance, when a guest praises a host by saying that the host's *djambe* makes him such a fine person—that only a vague translation, like "special energy," would be appropriate. .... Thus the translation of *djambe* as "witchcraft" risks primitivizing a much richer cosmology. (Geschiere 1997: 13)

In the case of the Maka, it is particularly notable that people are most often accused of using their *djambe* due to jealousy they feel over the success of a kinsperson. Geschiere describes Maka culture as involving "strongly egalitarian overtones," in the sense that all men (note the explicit gender inequality, which Geschiere largely ignores) are born as equals and remains equal to one another. However, Maka men are also constantly striving for notability among their peers, especially in the form of honorific titles. *Djambe*, in this sense, is the embodiment of a personal ambition that exists among equals who are nevertheless consistently caught up with striving for honorability among one another. The existence of *djambe* is particularly problematic among kinspeople, in relation to whom one is normally compelled to forego even attempts at symbolic status. Having kin means having allies and support in one's efforts to gain status, but can also mean that feelings of rivalry that emerge within one's kin network must be repressed. "Discourse on *djambe* expresses the frightening awareness that there is in fact inequality, and thus jealousy, in the interior of the family—that is, between people with whom one must live and work" (Geschiere 1997: 42). Although Geschiere does not explicitly make this sort of psychological argument, the structure of relationships within kin networks would appear to deeply embed *djambe* discourse into the unconscious lives of people living in Maka communities.

94   There is good reason to think that this discourse is also highly functional within the national community at large. National politicians generally accrue their power by mobilizing a local network of supporters, which necessarily requires the participation of their kinsfolk. Well-connected entrepreneurial farmers require the participation of local communities as workers and allies, again requiring the involvement of kin networks in one way or another. So while politicians and entrepreneurial farmers frequently operate in and through national channels, they also remain rooted in local communities and connected to their kin networks. The judgments of people who live in those communities are consistently couched in terms of witchcraft—that is, they involve accusations that the wealthy and powerful have misused their *djambe* to establish their position.

Because of the connections between local communities and the nation-state, Geschiere argues that notions of witchcraft can actually be used to "reestablish the idea of basic equality" that is threatened by the very presence of large-scale national institutions. That is to say, prototypically local notions such as *djambe* have an important role in mediating forms of inequality on the national level. Geschiere emphasizes the fact that witchcraft discourse has actually grown alongside these large-scale institutions. Indeed, one of the most striking aspects of Geschiere's ethnography is the manner in which he represents political elites—ostensibly among the most modern citizens of the nation-state—as deeply concerned about both being the target of witchcraft accusations and the target of witchcraft itself. Similar observations about ostensibly modern people being concerned about witchcraft can be made for cases involving those wealthy entrepreneurial farmers who specialize in cash crops such as cocoa, and thereby have immediate access to wealth flowing in from overseas (Geschiere 1997: 141–42).

Witchcraft discourse is, according to this sort of argument, ultimately about the kind of "profound distrust of power" that can be reinforced by "the emergence of new forms of power and wealth that seem to be beyond the reach of local communities" (Geschiere 1997: 133–34). Taking the argument of local–national linkage one step farther, the anthropologist Ralph Austen has argued that the type of witchcraft discourse analyzed by Geschiere is emblematic of an inequality not only within African nation-states, but also between rich countries outside of Africa and an Africa continent subject as a whole to "marginalized domination." For Austen (1993: 105), witchcraft is a "telling, truthful insight into the modern experience of the continent," which may require the "self-proclaimed universal logic of capitalist discourse ... to subject itself to the moral and cultural interrogations of a new genre of witch finders" operating on the local level. In my opinion, this sort of broad characterization of the experience of an entire continent needs to be taken with a grain of salt. By contrast, Comaroff and Comaroff offer a somewhat more carefully crafted conclusion: "Witchcraft is a finely calibrated gauge of the impact of global cultural and economic   **95** forces on local relations, on money and markets, on the abstraction and alienation of 'indigenous' values and meanings" (1993: 223).

Anxiety and the Cosmetic Body

In the previous section, I hinted at some of the ways in which inequality helps to shape people's unconscious motivations. Desire and anxiety, ambition and narcissism are all conditioned by personal experiences of inequality. The theme of anxiety is particularly important for an analysis of the work of the ethnographer Alexander Edmonds (2010), whose project centers on *plástica* (plastic surgery) in Brazil. To put this project in context, several things are notable. First, Brazil has unusually high rates of plastic surgery—on a per capita basis, it is surpassed only by South Korea. Second, plastic surgery in Brazil is available through both private and public clinics. Poor people who wish to receive plastic surgery must endure wait times of several years, but can usually receive a wide variety of procedures at no cost. This is in part because health care has been described as a right in Brazil since the late 1980s. While inadequate funding can make this right less than secure, it does allow at least for the development of a public clinic infrastructure. In addition, Brazil's public clinics serve as training grounds for plastic surgeons from Brazil and around the world. While this means that procedures are not always carried out by experienced surgeons, it does mean they are widely available at low cost.

The public provision of *plástica* would hardly matter without a willing clientele. The overwhelmingly female clients who visit free public clinics for the purposes of cosmetic enhancement describe such procedures as essential to the maintenance of *auto-estima* (self-esteem). Here is one of Edmonds's informants, a maid from Rio de Janeiro: "I did plastic surgery not because of physical, but psychological, discomfort. I was married seven years, but to start another relationships you think, will someone like me, accept my defects? This messes with your interior. I didn't put in an implant to exhibit myself, to call attention of men on the street, but to feel better.

It wasn't simple vanity, but necessary aesthetic surgery. A necessary vanity. Surgery improves a woman's *auto-estima*" (2010: 46).

In the words of two feminist authors, cosmetic surgery is "a way of dealing with the unwanted intrusion of the body into consciousness" (Heyes and Jones 2009: 4). The unique anxiety of displeasure with one's own body can be erased—as if by magic.

Looking for a broader context that informs the use of *plástica* by poor Brazilians, Edmonds points to the popular culture of the annual *Carnaval*, which famously celebrates pleasure and unbridled pageantry. It is particularly interesting to note the association of *Carnaval* with the inversion of social hierarchies and norms, such that poor Brazilians celebrate themselves as the center of the spectacle. In this sense, it is possible to see the widespread use of *plástica* as a rebuke to a deeply inegalitarian society divided between rich and poor. At *Carnaval*, the poor are the center of attention and attraction.

Much of life happens outside *Carnaval*, of course, so Edmonds must also look for an explanation of how the use of *plástica* in the public health system makes sense year round. A famous surgeon among his informants insists that "the poor have a right to be beautiful," and asks, "Faced with an aesthetic defect, don't the poor suffer as much as the rich?" The "right to be beautiful" has a kind of leveling effect, allowing each person to prize her or his *auto-estima* as an end in itself. Aware that plastic surgery is relevant to women because they are constantly assessed (and encouraged to assess themselves) based on their appearance, Edmonds (2010: 236) nevertheless pushes aside an explicitly feminist analysis of plastic surgery, arguing that "applying the patriarchal analytical lens to beauty practices across cultures must be balanced by attention to local economic pressures and aspirations for mobility." He further argues that "for some workers and consumers on the margins of the market economy, physical allure can be an asset that actually seems to disrupt the class hierarchies that pervade many other aspects of their lives" (250).

As it so happens, I think that Edmonds's explanation of *plástica* as a practice that basically functions to engender equality is misguided. I agree with his conclusion that it is a mistake to moralize about plastic surgery; body modification does not simply replace the natural with the artificial, and there is nothing morally superior in an unmodified outward appearance. Like any form of cosmetic modification, *plástica* creates a new sort of embodied self—a "social skin," in the words of the anthropologist Terrence Turner. Nonetheless, it is equally clear that the underlying gendered standards of beauty present in Brazilian practices surrounding plastic surgery are themselves highly inegalitarian. *Plástica* in Brazil overwhelmingly centers on the reinforcement of standards of beauty that are not freely chosen by individual women, but rather imposed by the force of culture at large. Moreover, anxious concern about appearance is imposed more on women than on men. As the analysis of intersectionality in Chapter 4 suggests, any liberation from class hierarchies achieved through the consumption of *plástica* should not be taken as a simultaneous liberation from gender and ethnic hierarchies surrounding the imposed aesthetics of bodies.[1]

To begin to deconstruct Edmonds's account of *plástica* as a form of liberation from economic inequality, it is helpful to look at the following passage from the last page of his book *Pretty Modern*: "Beauty can occupy a similar position in the social imaginary for girls that soccer does for boys. While boys living in poverty often dream of becoming professional athletes, many girls in poor communities have the equally impossible dream of becoming fashion models. In both fantasies, the invisibility of poverty is best negated by media visibility [i.e., becoming a star]. When access to education is limited, the body—relative to the mind—becomes a more important basis for identity as well as a source of power" (2010: 252).

This passage problematically asserts a parallel between two different fantasies. While the fantasy outlined for boys is one where the body is actively engaged in athletic achievement, the fantasy outlined for girls involves a passive body that is consumed by the implicitly male gaze of the public at large. Poor boys and poor girls alike suffer from economic inequality, but Edmonds's own depiction of the very fantasy of redemption from this suffering places poor girls in a passive and inferior position to poor boys. If our analysis of inequality is reduced solely to an analysis of the "class hierarchies" represented by Edmonds, we run the danger of believing that a liberation from class hierarchy means a liberation from hierarchy per se.

Health and Inequality

In the previous section, we saw one way in which bodily experiences matter—the way that people see themselves is conditioned by their experience of social life. Quite clearly, however, bodies also matter as the material basis for experience. In the introduction, I noted that this book would be devoted to the kinds of concerns that can be described through ethnographic fieldwork. In large part, this means putting aside concerns of biological anthropology—for example, the question of whether the process of human evolution disposes us in some concrete way toward equality and reciprocity. This is an interesting question, but hardly something that can be addressed on an ethnographic basis. However, what can be addressed

---

1   The mention of ethnic hierarchies refers to another important question discussed by Edmonds, having to do with whether or not plastic surgery in Brazil validates the stereotypical appearance of white ethnicities as superior to black and brown ones.

is the way that the medical treatment of bodies affects and is affected by forms of inequality.

In recent years, anthropologists and public health scholars have focused with increasing intensity on the relationship between health and inequality. Some good examples of this are the attempts to describe the "systemic exclusion" of poor women in Africa from skilled medical care during childbirth. In an article in *Medical Anthropology Quarterly*, Sydney A. Spangler describes how processes of social exclusion and the economics of health care produce unequal outcomes for women in the Kilombero Valley of south-central Tanzania. Women in Tanzania face a 1-in-23 chance of dying from obstetric causes in their lifetime, compared to a 1-in-4,300 chance for women in industrialized countries (Spangler 2011: 481). Poor women in Tanzania face even higher risks. As Spangler points out, these risks are mediated by local cultural categories such as *wanaweza* (the "ables"—i.e., the modern and relatively well-off) and *hawawezi* (the "unables"—i.e., the destitute and poor). The way that women are interpreted by others as belonging to one or the other of these categories matters to their health outcomes. "Women stood different chances of exclusion based on how they were assessed by those with authority and by society at large. People of every position describe facility providers as exhibiting *dharau* (scorn, devaluing) for women determined to be *hawawezi*" (Spangler 2011: 491).

These sorts of social exclusions dovetail with the economics of childbirth. While obstetric care at state-run clinics is meant to be free for all, women are increasingly expected to provide their own medical materials—such as soap, basins, razors, needles, medicine, and even kerosene for the clinic's lamps. They are also expected to provide a tip, or *asante* ("thank you"), for the medical provider. Poor women struggle with these burdens and face stern rebukes and refusals of care when they cannot carry them out. Spangler refers to medical care in Tanzania as an "emergent capitalist system," where prices are erratic and often disguised by notions of self-support and gratitude toward caregivers. The bottom line, however, is that "socioeconomic inequalities make their way into women's bodies" as the state slowly decreases funding for clinics and turns a blind eye toward the way that care is actually delivered (491). In related work, Spangler and her co-authors (Spangler, Barry, and Sibley 2014) have suggested that programs that are highly targeted toward poor women can help to turn the tide of these rising inequalities. I would note, however, that such programs would potentially run up against the "state of the poor" dilemma described in Chapter 6.

A more systematic argument regarding inequality and well-being has been made by the epidemiologists Richard G. Wilkinson and Kate Pickett. In *The Spirit Level: Why More Equal Societies Almost Always Do Better*,

Wilkinson and Pickett argue that unequal rich countries (such as the United Kingdom or the United States) have worse outcomes that equal rich countries (such as Denmark or Japan) across a series of variables— including mental health, drug abuse, life expectancy, obesity, violence, and imprisonment. Arguing that social ills are not caused merely by the poverty of individual people, they quote the anthropologist Marshall Sahlins, stating that "poverty is not a certain small amount of goods, nor is it just a relation between means and ends; above all it is a relation between people. . . . Poverty is a social status" (Wilkinson and Pickett 2011: 15). The point of this definition is that poor health outcomes and high levels of social problems are associated with the low social status that the *relatively* poor have in highly unequal societies. Wilkinson and Pickett argue that inequality gets "under the skin" and produces higher levels of anxiety and lower levels of self-esteem. They analyze the culture of self-promotion that they see in the United States, for example, as the result of widespread "social evaluation anxieties" present across all socio-economic groups. Inequality is *in the body* or *under the skin* in the sense that individual people feel its effects in their biological constitution, rather than through any strictly abstract participation in social categories.

CONCLUSION

I began this book with two very simple propositions: first, that inequality mat- ters, and second, that we are frequently called upon to examine inequality from a global perspective. We have seen how anthropologists have variously grappled with inequality on local and global levels. We have seen how inequality can be systematic, and how different forms of inequality can reinforce one another. To quote again from the sociologist Sylvia Walby (see Chapter 1), there is no "primary form of inequality." Instead, we are struck by a world in which inequalities are multiple and overlapping.

Capitalist economies have been crucial to the process of globalization, and so we also find that they are very often relevant to the formation of global inequalities. Nation-states play a crucial role here, as well. Our concerns about inequality are frequently bounded by the nation-state, which functions both to contain inequalities within nations and maintain inequalities between nations. We can also speak about particularly global forms of gender and ethnic inequality, as well as unequal treatment based on sexual orientation.

Regardless of the particular forms of inequality that we might analyze, there remains a deeper point regarding inequality and ethnographic methods. Ethnography is a social-scientific method based on relationships with other people. Once we are concerned with relationships, we are inevitably concerned with inequality as well. The result is that, even when anthropologists are not directly addressing inequality, it is possible to read their ethnographic accounts as intimately linked to this theme. Indeed, I would challenge each student to do this—in another course, or even outside of the university, to read an ethnography and think about how ethnographic engagement with the case at hand makes the theme of inequality noticeable. Our concerns with inequality are not always explicit, but they are almost always present.

I have stated that inequality is a problem. It is worth adding here that there is no perfect form of equality that will relieve us of this problem. If nothing else, what ethnography teaches us is that inequality is something that we will continually discover in new forms. We can hope that this ongoing process of discovery will help to make the world a more egalitarian place, but we should not hope to ever completely put this process behind us.

Likewise, globalization is a process without an end point. It is, in fact, a good thing that there is no completely *globalized world* for us to look forward to. For some decades to come, the world will almost certainly become more integrated, and most people's lives will almost certainly become more closely interrelated. In this case, then, what ethnography teaches us is that we must engage with this process from within the local contexts in which we encounter it. There will always be local sites of ethnographic meaning, even as our anthropological concerns about these sites become themselves more interrelated.

102

APPENDIX 1: ADDITIONAL READINGS AND FILMS

Following is a list of suggested further readings. Some of these readings
are discussed in the text, while others have been suggested to complement
material discussed and cited there.

CHAPTER 1

Geertz, Clifford. 1968. "Thinking as a Moral Act: Ethical Dimensions of
Anthropological Fieldwork in the New States." *Antioch Review* 28 (2): 139–58.
Also in *Available Light: Anthropological Reflections on Philosophical Topics* by Clifford
Geertz. Princeton, NJ: Princeton University Press, 2000.

Milanovic, Branko. 2010. "Two Students of Inequality." Vignette 1.10 in *The Haves
and the Have-Nots: A Brief and Idiosyncratic History of Global Inequality*, 83–91.
New York: Basic Books.

Povinelli, Elizabeth. 1998. "The State of Shame: Australian Multiculturalism and
the Crisis of Indigenous Citizenship." *Critical Inquiry* 24 (2): 575–610.

Sen, Amartya. 2002. "How to Judge Globalism." *The American Prospect* 13 (1):
1–14. Also in *The Politics of Globalization: A Reader* by Mark Kesselman. Boston:
Wadsworth, 2006.

Trouillot, Michel-Rolph. 2003. "A Fragmented Globality." Chapter 3 in *Global
Transformations: Anthropology and the Modern World*. New York: Palgrave
Macmillan.

CHAPTER 2

Ferguson, James. 2006. "The Anti-Politics Machine." Chapter 11 in *The Anthropology
of State: A Reader*, edited by Aradhana Sharma and Akhil Gupta. Malden, MA:
Blackwell Publishing.

Hickel, Jason. 2012. "Social Engineering and Revolutionary Consciousness:
Domestic Transformations in Colonial South Africa." *History and Anthropology*
23 (3): 301–22.

Trouillot, Michel-Rolph. 2003. "Anthropology and the Savage Slot." Chapter 1 in
Global Transformations: Anthropology and the Modern World. New York: Palgrave
Macmillan.

Tsing, Anna. 2000. "The Global Situation." *Cultural Anthropology* 15 (3): 327–60.

Wallerstein, Immanuel Maurice. 2004. "The Modern World-System as a Capitalist
World-Economy: Production, Surplus-Value and Polarization." Chapter 2 in
World-Systems Analysis: An Introduction. Durham, NC: Duke University Press.

CHAPTER 3

Fischer, Edward F., and Peter Blair Benson. 2007. "Broccoli and Desire." *Antipode* 39 (5): 800–20.

Graeber, David. 2014. "On the Experience of Moral Confusion." Chapter 1 in *Debt: The First 5,000 Years*. Brooklyn, NY: Melville House.

Hann, Chris, and Keith Hart. 2011. "Unequal Development." Chapter 6 in *Economic Anthropology*. London: Polity.

Harvey, David. 2005. "Uneven Geographical Developments." Chapter 4 in *A Brief History of Neoliberalism*. Oxford: Oxford University Press.

Holmes, Douglas R., and George E. Marcus. 2008. "Collaboration Today and the Re-imagination of the Classic Scene of Fieldwork Encounter." *Collaborative Anthropologies* 1 (1): 81–101.

Life and Debt. 2001. Documentary film directed by Stephanie Black. New Yorker Films.

Rapley, John. 2004. "Inequality and Instability." Chapter 1 in *Globalization and Inequality: Neoliberalism's Downward Spiral*. Boulder, CO: Lynne Rienner Publishers.

Stiglitz, Joseph E. 2007. "Making Trade Fair." Chapter 3 in *Making Globalization Work*. New York: W.W. Norton & Company.

CHAPTER 4

Buch, Elana D. 2013. "Senses of Care: Embodying Inequality and Sustaining Personhood in the Home Care of Older Adults in Chicago." *American Ethnologist* 40 (4): 637–50.

Dasgupta, Samir. 2009. "Globalization Politics with Women's Empowerment." Chapter 10 in *Politics of Globalization*, edited by Samir Dasgupta and Jan Nederveen Pieterse. New Delhi: SAGE.

Devereaux, Leslie. 1987. "Gender Difference and the Relations of Inequality in Zinacantan." Chapter 3 in *Dealing with Inequality*, edited by Marilyn Strathern. Cambridge: Cambridge University Press.

Ho, Karen. 2009. "Disciplining Investment Bankers, Disciplining the Economy: Wall Street's Institutional Culture of Crisis and the Downsizing of 'Corporate America.'" *American Anthropologist* 111 (2): 177–89.

Ho, Karen. 2009. "Wall Street's Orientation: Exploitation, Empowerment and the Politics of Hard Work." Chapter 2 in *Liquidated: An Ethnography of Wall Street*. Durham, NC: Duke University Press.

Krugman, Paul. 2014. "Why We're in a New Gilded Age." *The New York Review of Books*, May 8.

Lutz, Catherine. 2014. "The US Car Colossus and the Production of Inequality." *American Ethnologist* 41 (2): 232–45.

Piketty, Thomas, and Emmanuel Saez. 2014. "Inequality in the Long Run." *Science* 344 (6186): 838–43.

CHAPTER 5

Bartels, Larry M. 2009. "Do Americans Care about Inequality?" Chapter 5 in *Unequal Democracy: The Political Economy of the New Gilded Age*. Princeton, NJ: Princeton University Press.

De Genova, Nicholas. 2010. "The Queer Politics of Migration: Reflections on 'Illegality' and Incorrigibility." *Studies in Social Justice* 4 (2): 101–26.

Engelke, Matthew. 1999. "'We Wondered What Human Rights He Was Talking About': Human Rights, Homosexuality and the Zimbabwe International Book Fair." *Critique of Anthropology* 19 (3): 289–314.

Reilly, Niamh. 2009. "Human Rights, Gender and Contested Meanings." Chapter 2 in *Women's Human Rights*. London: Polity.

Stiglitz, Joseph. 2012. "Justice for All? How Inequality Is Eroding the Rule of Law." Chapter 7 in *The Price of Inequality*. New York: Penguin.

Wacquant, Loïc. 2005. "Race as Civic Felony." *International Social Science Journal* 57 (183): 127–42.

CHAPTER 6

Dubbeld, Bernard. 2013. "Envisioning Governance: Expectations and Estrangements of Transformed Rule in Glendale, South Africa." *Africa* 83 (3): 492–512.

Edin, Kathryn, and Laura Lein. 1997. "Single Mothers, Welfare and Low-Wage Work." Chapter 1 in *Making Ends Meet: How Single Mothers Survive Welfare and Low-Wage Work*. New York: Russell Sage Foundation.

Eger, Talita Jabs, and Arlei Sander Damo. 2014. "Money and Morality in the Bolsa Família." *Vibrant: Virtual Brazilian Anthropology* 11 (1): 250–84.

Gupta, Akhil. 2012. "The State and the Politics of Poverty." Chapter 2 in *Red Tape: Bureaucracy, Structural Violence, and Poverty in India*. Durham, NC: Duke University Press.

Higham, Rob, and Alpa Shah. 2013. "Affirmative Action and Political Economic Transformations: Secondary Education, Indigenous People, and the State in Jharkhand, India." *Focaal* 2013 (65): 80–93.

Mitchell, Sean T. "Space, Sovereignty, Inequality: Interpreting the Explosion of Brazil's VLS Rocket." *Journal of Latin American and Caribbean Anthropology* 18 (3): 395–412.

Morton, Gregory Duff. 2014. "Protest Before the Protests: The Unheard Politics of a Welfare Panic in Brazil." *Anthropological Quarterly* 87 (3): 925–33.

Sen, Amartya. 1993. "Capability and Well-being." In *The Quality of Life*, edited by Martha Craven Nussbaum and Amartya Kumar Sen. Oxford: Clarendon Press.

CHAPTER 7

Beynon, Louise. 2004. "Dilemmas of the Heart: Rural Working Women and Their Hopes for the Future." Chapter 4 in *On the Move: Women and Rural-to-Urban Migration in Contemporary China*, edited by Arianna M. Gaetano and Tamara Jacka. New York: Columbia University Press.

Hairong, Yan. 2003. "Neoliberal Governmentality and Neohumanism: Organizing Suzhi/Value Flow through Labor Recruitment Networks." *Cultural Anthropology* 18 (4): 493–523.

Hardt, Michael, and Antonio Negri. 2011. "The Fight for 'Real Democracy' at the Heart of Occupy Wall Street." *Foreign Affairs* 11: 2011.

Nugent, David. 2012. "Commentary: Democracy, Temporalities of Capitalism, and Dilemmas of Inclusion in Occupy Movements." *American Ethnologist* 39 (2): 280–83.

Sitrin, Marina. 2006. *Horizontalism: Voices of Popular Power in Argentina*. Oakland, CA: AK Press.

The Take. Documentary film by Naomi Klein and Avi Lewis. First Run Features/ Icarus Films (2004).

Wright, Teresa. 2010. "Introduction." Chapter 1 in *Accepting Authoritarianism: State-Society Relations in China's Reform Era*. Stanford, CA: Stanford University Press.

CHAPTER 8

Callan, Alyson. 2007. "'What Else Do We Bengalis Do?' Sorcery, Overseas Migration, and the New Inequalities in Sylhet, Bangladesh." *Journal of the Royal Anthropological Institute* 13 (2): 331–43.

Demerath, Peter, Jill Lynch, and Mario Davidson. 2008. "Dimensions of Psychological Capital in a US Suburb and High School: Identities for Neoliberal Times." *Anthropology & Education Quarterly* 39 (3): 270–92.

Edmonds, Alexander. 2007. "'The Poor Have the Right to be Beautiful': Cosmetic Surgery in Neoliberal Brazil." *Journal of the Royal Anthropological Institute* 13 (2): 363–81.

Rylko-Bauer, Barbara, and Paul Farmer. 2002. "Managed Care or Managed Inequality? A Call for Critiques of Market-Based Medicine." *Medical Anthropology Quarterly* 16 (4): 476–502.

Smith, Daniel Jordan. 2001. "Ritual Killing, 419, and Fast Wealth: Inequality and the Popular Imagination in Southeastern Nigeria." *American Ethnologist* 28 (4): 803–26.

Spangler, Sydney A. 2011. "'To Open Oneself Is a Poor Woman's Trouble': Embodied Inequality and Childbirth in South-Central Tanzania." *Medical Anthropology Quarterly* 25 (4): 479–98.

APPENDIX 2: STUDY AND ESSAY QUESTIONS

The following is a list of questions available for use in class discussion or as essay prompts. The questions pertain to the readings cited in Appendix 1.

CHAPTER 1

In "Thinking as a Moral Act," Clifford Geertz argues that detachment from the people one is studying is a crucial part of ethnographic fieldwork but that this detachment is "laboriously earned and precariously maintained" (39). Do you agree with this assessment?

In "How to Judge Globalism," Amartya Sen argues that "it is not adequate to ask whether international inequality is getting marginally larger or smaller" (5). Merely making the poor of the world slightly less poor is not, in Sen's argument, morally adequate. How do you think we should judge the contributions of globalization to changes in global inequality? How and why does your point of view differ or coincide with Sen's own?

In her article "The State of Shame," Elizabeth Povinelli argues that the Australian "court and state construct native title as a legitimate part of state multiculturalism only to plough it into the ground of a new, transcendental, monocultural nation" (579). Explain her argument, and argue the degree to which all attempts to create multiculturalism will be to the advantage of the already dominant cultural group.

CHAPTER 2

In her article "The Global Situation," Anna Tsing argues that anthropology runs the danger of falling prey to "globalist wishes and fantasies" (330). How does Tsing support this proposition, and what do you think of her assessment?

In his article "Social Engineering and Revolutionary Consciousness," Jason Hickel argues that African cultural groups adopted European ideologies of equality to fight against colonial exploitation. What do you think that this adoption of European ideas to fight European colonial domination says about the process of liberation from colonialism, as well as the possibilities for community in a postcolonial nation?

In his book *The Anti-Politics Machine* (see selection in *The Anthropology of the State: A Reader*), James Ferguson argues that development projects help to "de-politicize" poverty. Does this mean that poverty is necessarily a political issue? If not, how can you defend a technocratic approach to poverty against Ferguson's critique? If so, how can poverty be described as a political issue in either national or international contexts?

CHAPTER 3

In their article "Broccoli and Desire," Edward F. Fischer and Peter Blair Benson argue that poor Mayan farmers in Mexico should not be described as exploited, but rather as participating in a "patchwork of desires, interests, and investments in which expectations and opportunities are mediated by geographies of class, capital, and individual subjectivities" (802). Does this argument make any sense? In other words, do Fischer and Benson give us any way to understand this "patchwork" except through apparently random connections? Analyze carefully the strengths and weaknesses of their argument.

In their article "Collaboration Today and the Re-imagination of the Classic Scene of Fieldwork Encounter," Douglas Holmes and George E. Marcus make an argument that might be problematic. What do you think are the advantages and disadvantages of collaborating with privileged informants from outside the anthropological profession?

In the first chapter of his book *Debt*, David Graeber argues that "we don't know what debt is" (5)—that is, that most people don't understand that debt relationships are not simply about the debtor's requirement to repay. Do you agree with this statement? Explain your answer.

CHAPTER 4

In her article "Senses of Care," Elana Buch argues that care for elderly people often "generates and reproduces systematic, intersecting forms of structural inequality" (638). Her argument is a powerful one, but it leaves one crucial premise unaddressed: Are the relationships described in this article ones of genuine caring? If so, can a relationship of genuine caring truly generate inequality? Does doing so require that the people who care—in this case, these people are tellingly poor and minority women—be willing to participate in the creation of their own inequality? What does this say about my argument in the first chapter that inequality is about differences in things that people value? If people are willing to sacrifice their own well-being, does this mean that they remain equal in some way with the people they sacrifice themselves for?

In her article "Disciplining Investment Bankers, Disciplining the Economy," Karen Ho argues that investment bankers experience their own precarious employment in terms of their "attempt to perform and actualize their model of what the market is" (186). That is to say, these bankers use the insecurity of their own position as a way to explain their own participation in corporate restructuring outside the bank. What does this say to you about the larger culture of business? Does the way that elite actors manage their own insecurity tell us anything about the existence of inequality in a precarious labor market?

CHAPTER 5

In "Race as Civic Felony," Loïc Wacquant argues that racial inequality in the United States involves a "centuries-old association of blackness with criminality" (128). Insofar as this is the case, Wacquant's argument implies that within the legal system in the United States, African American people are likely to be interpreted as criminals regardless of the actual facts of any given case. What do you think of this argument? What does your conclusion about Wacquant's argument tell us about the possibility of racial equality in the United States?

In his article "'We Wondered What Human Rights He Was Talking About,'" Matthew Engelke describes himself as "an anthropologist interested in human rights" and hopeful of pursuing "the kind of positive change that human rights work aims for" (290). Does this mean he is for or against human rights laws? Does his ethnographic description in this article give us reason to support or oppose the existence of formalized national laws protecting human rights?

In "The Queer Politics of Migration," Nicholas De Genova argues that "to conduct research related to the undocumented noncitizens of a particular nation-state from the unexamined standpoint of its citizens, then, involves the kind of uncritical ethnocentrism that is, by definition, a perversion of anthropology's putative aims as a distinctive mode of inquiry" (422). Do you think that De Genova's article offers us a reasonable means to avoid ethnocentrism? Indeed, do you think that questioning cultural scripts of "illegality" is a good way to avoid ethnocentric bias within anthropology itself?

CHAPTER 6

In "Affirmative Action and Political Economic Transformations," Rob Higham and Alpa Shah describe the gradual tendency for the Indian welfare state to turn into a "state of the poor" (89). Do you think this is a tendency inherent to welfare states? Why or why not?

In "Protest Before the Protests," Gregory Duff Morton frames universal welfare payments in Brazil as a possible "wage for housework" and even hints that such a wage is a "just" demand (931). What sorts of arguments can be made for state welfare payments as wages for housework? Are these good or bad arguments?

CHAPTER 7

In "Neoliberal Governmentality and Neohumanism," Yan Hairong argues that the category of *suzhi* involves a "valorization and abstraction of human consciousness for market and development" (494). What does this imply about the ability of economic markets to organize human consciousness? Use Hairong's case to explain your answer.

In their editorial "The Fight for 'Real Democracy' at the Heart of Occupy Wall Street," Michael Hardt and Antonio Negri argue that this protest centers on a concern that politicians in the United States today "more clearly represent the banks and the creditors" than they do ordinary people. They contrast this with "real democracy," involving "frequent assemblies of participatory decision-making structures." What do you think of this vision of "real democracy"? Is it viable and meaningful in the world outside of protest encampments such as Occupy Wall Street? You may want to support your argument with examples from Marina Sitrin's research on "horizontalism" or from the film *The Take*.

110   CHAPTER 8

In "'What Else Do We Bengalis Do?'" Allison Callan argues that some people invoke a "sorcery diagnosis" to save face for their own lack of wealth or status. This is particularly the case in light of new inequalities brought on by labor migration to more wealthy countries. What do you think of this explanation for the growth of sorcery accusations in Callan's fieldsite? Does her result support the argument that modern economic transformations can actually encourage the growth of witchcraft accusations?

In "Dimensions of Psychological Capital in a US Suburb and High School," Peter Demerath and his co-authors argue that students in a high school situated in a wealthy community tend to accrue "psychological capital" in large amounts. In an important sense, what these authors are arguing is that self-assuredness and confidence are commodities that can be acquired within particular educational institutions. Does it make sense to say that these kinds of internal, psychological attributes actually have economic value? If so, what does this imply for educational inequalities in the United States and other similar countries? If not, what would be a better vocabulary for describing the relationship between wealth, self-confidence, and education?

REFERENCES

Amin, Samir. 1976. *Unequal Exchange*. New York: Monthly Review Press.

Appadurai, Arjun. 1996. *Modernity at Large: Cultural Dimensions of Globalization*. Minneapolis: University of Minnesota Press.

Augé, Marc. 2013. *L'anthropologue et le monde global*. Paris: Armand Colin.

Austen, Ralph A. 1993. "The Moral Economy of Witchcraft: An Essay in Comparative History." In *Modernity and Its Malcontents: Ritual and Power in Postcolonial Africa*, edited by Jean Comaroff and John Comaroff, 89–110. Chicago: University of Chicago Press.

Bayart, Jean-François. 2004. *Le gouvernement du monde: une critique politique de la globalisation*. Paris: Fayard.

Bhabha, Homi K. 1994. *The Location of Culture*. New York: Psychology Press.

Biddle, Bruce Jesse, and David C. Berliner. 2003. *What Research Says about Unequal Funding for Schools in America*. San Francisco: WestEd.

Bonvillain, Nancy. 2010. *Cultural Anthropology*, 2nd ed. New York: Prentice Hall.

Borneman, John. 1986. "Emigres as Bullets/Immigration as Penetration Perceptions of the Marielitos." *Journal of Popular Culture* 20 (3): 73–92. http://dx.doi.org/10.1111/j.0022-3840.1986.2003_73.x.

Braudel, Fernand. 1979. *Civilization and Capitalism, 15th–18th Century*. Volume 2: *The Wheels of Commerce*. New York: Harper and Row.

Brewer, John. 1990. *The Sinews of Power: War, Money, and the English State, 1688–1783*. Cambridge, MA: Harvard University Press.

Brodkin, Karen. 1998. "Race, Class, and Gender: The Metaorganization of American Capitalism." *Transforming Anthropology* 7 (2): 46–57. http://dx.doi.org/10.1525/tran.1998.7.2.46.

Brooks, Clem, and Jeff Manza. 2008. *Why Welfare States Persist: The Importance of Public Opinion in Democracies*. Chicago: University of Chicago Press.

Buch, Elana D. 2013. "Senses of Care: Embodying Inequality and Sustaining Personhood in the Home Care of Older Adults in Chicago." *American Ethnologist* 40 (4): 637–50. http://dx.doi.org/10.1111/amet.12044.

Cammarota, Julio. 2008. *Sueños Americanos: Barrio Youth Negotiating Social and Cultural Identities*. Tucson: University of Arizona Press.

Carrier, James G. 1998. "Introduction." In *Virtualism: A New Political Economy*, edited by James G. Carrier and Daniel Miller, 1–24. Oxford: Berg.

Chang, Ha-Joon. 2002. *Kicking Away the Ladder: Development Strategy in Historical Perspective*. London: Anthem Press.

Clark, Gregory. 2007. *A Farewell to Alms: A Brief Economic History of the World.* Princeton, NJ: Princeton University Press.

Comaroff, Jean, and John L. Comaroff, eds. 1993. "Introduction." In *Modernity and its Malcontents: Ritual and Power in Postcolonial Africa*, xi–xxxvii. Chicago: University of Chicago Press.

Comaroff, John L. 1989. "Images of Empire, Contests of Conscience: Models of Colonial Domination in South Africa." *American Ethnologist* 16 (4): 661–85. http://dx.doi.org/10.1525/ae.1989.16.4.02a00040.

Constable, Nicole. 2007. *Maid to Order in Hong Kong: Stories of Migrant Workers*, 2nd ed. Ithaca, NY: Cornell University Press.

Coutin, Susan Bibler. 2003. *The Culture of Protest: Religious Activism and the US Sanctuary Movement.* Boulder, CO: Westview Press.

Daley, Suzanne. 2013. "Danes Rethink a Welfare State Ample to a Fault." *New York Times*, April 20. Online edition.

Dasgupta, Samir. 2009. "Globalization Politics with Women's Empowerment." In *Politics of Globalization*, edited by Samir Dasgupta and Jan Nederveen Pieterse, 242–67. New Delhi: SAGE. http://dx.doi.org/10.4135/9788132108283.n11.

De Genova, Nicholas P. 2002. "Migrant 'Illegality' and Deportability in Everyday Life." *Annual Review of Anthropology* 31 (1): 419–47. http://dx.doi.org/10.1146/annurev.anthro.31.040402.085432.

Demerath, Peter. 2009. *Producing Success: The Culture of Personal Advancement in an American High School.* Chicago: University of Chicago Press. http://dx.doi.org/10.7208/chicago/9780226142425.001.0001.

De Vries, Jan. 2007. "Review of *A Farewell to Alms* by Gregory Clark." *Journal of Economic History* 68 (4): 1180–81.

Dirks, Nicholas B. 1997. "The Policing of Tradition: Colonialism and Anthropology in Southern India." *Comparative Studies in Society and History* 39 (1): 182–212.

Dubbeld, Bernard. 2013a. "How Social Security Becomes Social Insecurity: Unsettled Households, Crisis Talk and the Value of Grants in a KwaZulu-Natal Village." *Acta Juridica: Marriage, Land and Custom* 13: 197–217.

Dubbeld, Bernard. 2013b. "Envisioning Governance: Expectations and Estrangements of Transformed Rule in Glendale, South Africa." *Africa: Journal of the International Africa Institute* 83 (3): 492–512. http://dx.doi.org/10.1017/S0001972013000284.

Edmonds, Alexander. 2010. *Pretty Modern: Beauty, Sex, and Plastic Surgery in Brazil.* Durham, NC: Duke University Press. http://dx.doi.org/10.1215/9780822393115.

Eger, Talita Jabs, and Arlei Sander Damo. 2014. "Money and Morality in the Bolsa Família." *Vibrant: Virtual Brazilian Anthropology* 11, no. 1: 250–84.

Ehrenreich, Barbara, and Arlie Russell Hochschild. 2003. "Introduction." In *Global Woman: Nannies, Maids, and Sex Workers in the New Economy*, edited by Barbara Ehrenreich and Arlie Russell Hochschild, 1–13. New York: Macmillan.

Engelke, Matthew. 1999. "'We Wondered What Human Rights He Was Talking About': Human Rights, Homosexuality and the Zimbabwe International Book Fair." *Critique of Anthropology* 19 (3): 289–314. http://dx.doi.org/10.1177/0308275X9901900305.

Englund, Harri. 2006. *Prisoners of Freedom: Human Rights and the African Poor.* Berkeley: University of California Press.

Englund, Harri. 2011. *Human Rights and African Airwaves: Mediating Equality on the Chichewa Radio*. Bloomington: Indiana University Press.

Evans-Pritchard, E.E. 1940. *The Nuer*. Oxford: Oxford University Press.

Fallers, Lloyd A. 1973. *Inequality: Social Stratification Reconsidered*. Chicago: University of Chicago Press.

Ferguson, James. 1990. *The Anti-Politics Machine: "Development," Depoliticization, and Bureaucratic Power in Lesotho*. Cambridge: Cambridge University Press.

Fischer, Edward F., and Peter Blair Benson. 2006. *Broccoli and Desire: Global Connections and Maya Struggles in Postwar Guatemala*. Stanford, CA: Stanford University Press.

Fiske, Susan T. 2011. *Envy Up, Scorn Down: How Status Divides Us*. New York: Russell Sage Foundation.

Fox Piven, Frances. 1998. "Welfare Reform and the Economic and Cultural Reconstruction of Low Wage Labor Markets." *City & Society* 10 (1): 21–36. http://dx.doi.org/10.1525/city.1998.10.1.21.

Frank, Andre Gunder. 1966. *The Development of Underdevelopment*. Boston: New England Free Press.

Frank, Andre Gunder. 2004. "The 21st Century Will Be Asian." *The Nikkei Weekly* (Tokyo), August 5 (published in English). Quoted in *Globalization and Development in East Asia*, edited by Jan Nederveen Pieterse and Jongtae Kim, 2. London: Routledge.

Freeman, Carla. 2000. *High Tech and High Heels in the Global Economy: Women, Work, and Pink-collar Identities in the Caribbean*. Durham, NC: Duke University Press. http://dx.doi.org/10.1215/9780822380290.

Freeman, Carla. 2001. "Is Local: Global as Feminine: Masculine? Rethinking the Gender of Globalization." *Signs: Journal of Women in Culture and Society* 26 (4): 1007–37. http://dx.doi.org/10.1086/495646.

Freeman, Carla. 2007. "The 'Reputation' of Neoliberalism." *American Ethnologist* 34 (2): 252–67. http://dx.doi.org/10.1525/ae.2007.34.2.252.

Friedman, Eli. 2014. *Insurgency Trap: Labor Politics in Postsocialist China*. Ithaca, NY: Cornell University Press.

Friedman, Milton. 2009. *Capitalism and Freedom*. Chicago: University of Chicago Press.

Geertz, Clifford. 1963. "The Integrative Revolution: Primordial Sentiments and Civil Politics in the New States." In *Old Societies and New States*, edited by Clifford Geertz, 105–57. New York: Collier-Macmillan.

Geertz, Clifford. 1968. "Thinking as a Moral Act: Ethical Dimensions of Anthropological Fieldwork in the New States." *Antioch Review* 28 (2): 139–58. http://dx.doi.org/10.2307/4610913.

Geschiere, Peter. 1997. *The Modernity of Witchcraft: Politics and the Occult in Postcolonial Africa*. Charlottesville: University of Virginia Press.

Goldberg, Pinelopi Koujianou, and Nina Pavcnik. 2007. "Distributional Effects of Globalization in Developing Countries." *Journal of Economic Literature* 45 (1): 39–82. http://dx.doi.org/10.1257/jel.45.1.39.

Gonzales, Roberto G. 2011. "Learning to be Illegal: Undocumented Youth and Shifting Legal Contexts in the Transition to Adulthood." *American Sociological Review* 76 (4): 602–19. http://dx.doi.org/10.1177/0003122411411901.

Graeber, David. 2014. *Debt: The First 5,000 Years*, 2nd ed. New York: Melville House.

Griffin, Emma. 2010. *A Short History of the British Industrial Revolution*. London: Palgrave Macmillan.

Gupta, Akhil, and James Ferguson. 1992. "Beyond 'Culture': Space, Identity, and the Politics of Difference." *Cultural Anthropology* 7 (1): 6–23. http://dx.doi.org/10.1525/can.1992.7.1.02a00020.

Hacker, Jacob S., and Paul Pierson. 2011. *Winner-Take-All Politics: How Washington Made the Rich Richer—and Turned Its Back on the Middle Class*. New York: Simon and Schuster.

Hacker, Jacob S., Joe Soss, and Suzanne Mettler. 2007. "The New Politics of Inequality: A Policy-Centered Perspective." In *Remaking America: Democracy and Public Policy in and Age of Inequality*, edited by Joe Soss, Jacob S. Hacker, and Suzanne Mettler, 4–24. New York: Russell Sage Foundation.

Hairong, Yan. 2003. "Neoliberal Governmentality and Neohumanism: Organizing Suzhi/Value Flow through Labor Recruitment Networks." *Cultural Anthropology* 18 (4): 493–523. http://dx.doi.org/10.1525/can.2003.18.4.493.

Hanlon, Joseph, Armando Barrientos, and David Hulme. 2010. *Just Give Money to the Poor: The Development Revolution from the Global South*. Sterling, VA: Kumarian Press.

Harrison, Faye V. 1997. "The Gendered Politics and Violence of Structural Adjustment: A View from Jamaica." In *Situated Lives: Gender and Culture in Everyday Life*, edited by Louise Lamphere, Helena Ragoné, and Patricia Zavella, 451–68. London: Routledge.

Harvey, David. 2005. *A Brief History of Neoliberalism*. Oxford: Oxford University Press.

Held, David, Anthony McGrew, David Goldblatt, and Johanthan Perraton. 1999. *Global Transformations: Politics, Economics and Culture*. Stanford, CA: Stanford University Press.

Heyes, Cressida J., and Meredith Jones. 2009. "Cosmetic Surgery in the Age of Gender." In *Cosmetic Surgery: A Feminist Primer*, edited by Cressida J. Heyes and Meredith Rachael Jones, 1–17. Burlington, VT: Ashgate Publishing.

Hickel, Jason. 2012. "Social Engineering and Revolutionary Consciousness: Domestic Transformations in Colonial South Africa." *History and Anthropology* 23 (3): 301–22. http://dx.doi.org/10.1080/02757206.2012.697059.

Higham, Rob, and Alpa Shah. 2013. "Affirmative Action and Political Economic Transformations: Secondary Education, Indigenous People, and the State in Jharkhand, India." *Focaal* 2013 (65): 80–93. http://dx.doi.org/10.3167/fcl.2013.650108.

Hirst, Paul Q., Grahame Thompson, and Simon Bromley. 2009. *Globalization in Question*. Cambridge: Polity.

Holland, Dorothy C., and Margaret A. Eisenhart. 1990. *Educated in Romance: Women, Achievement, and College Culture*. Chicago: University of Chicago Press.

Holmes, Douglas R. 2009. "Economy of Words." *Cultural Anthropology* 24 (3): 381–419. http://dx.doi.org/10.1111/j.1548-1360.2009.01034.x.

Holmes, Douglas R., and George E. Marcus. 2008. "Collaboration Today and the Re-Imagination of the Classic Scene of Fieldwork Encounter." *Collaborative Anthropologies* 1 (1): 81–101. http://dx.doi.org/10.1353/cla.0.0003.

Holston, James. 1991. "Autoconstruction in Working-Class Brazil." *Cultural Anthropology* 6 (4): 447–65. http://dx.doi.org/10.1525/can.1991.6.4.02a00020.

Holston, James. 2008. *Insurgent Citizenship: Disjunctions of Democracy and Modernity in Brazil*. Princeton, NJ: Princeton University Press.

Hutchinson, Sharon Elaine. 2000. "Identity and Substance: The Broadening Bases of Relatedness among the Nuer of Southern Sudan." In *Cultures of Relatedness: New Approaches to the Study of Kinship*, edited by Janet Carsten, 55–72. Cambridge: Cambridge University Press.

Ibhawoh, Bonny. 2008. *Imperialism and Human Rights: Colonial Discourses of Rights and Liberties in African History*. Albany, NY: SUNY Press.

Ibrahim, Mahmood. 1990. *Merchant Capital and Islam*. Austin: University of Texas Press.

Jackson, Jean. 2009. "Report to the AAA Committee for Human Rights: The Awá of Southern Colombia: 'A Perfect Storm' of Violence." Available at: http://web .mit.edu/anthiopology/pdf/articles/jackson/jackson-Awa-CfHR-Report-2009.pdf (accessed 20 August 2015).

Jones, Emily. 2007. *Signing Away the Future: How Trade and Investment Agreements between Rich and Poor Countries Undermine Development*. Oxfam Briefing Paper. Oxford: Oxfam International.

Josephides, Lisette. 1985. *The Production of Inequality: Gender and Exchange among the Kewa*. London: Tavistock.

Josephides, Lisette. 1999. "Disengagement and Desire: The Tactics of Everyday Life." *American Ethnologist* 26 (1): 139–59. http://dx.doi.org/10.1525/ae.1999.26.1.139.

Kasrils, Ronnie. 2013. "How the ANC's Faustian Pact Sold Out South Africa's Poorest." *The Guardian*, June 24. Online edition.

Kipnis, Andrew. 2006. "*Suzhi*: A Keyword Approach." *China Quarterly* 186: 295–313. http://dx.doi.org/10.1017/S0305741006000166.

Korpi, Walter, and Joakim Palme. 1998. "The Paradox of Redistribution and Strategies of Equality: Welfare State Institutions, Inequality, and Poverty in the Western Countries." *American Sociological Review* 63 (5): 661–87. http://dx.doi .org/10.2307/2657333.

Kottak, Conrad Phillip. 2011. *Cultural Anthropology: Appreciating Cultural Diversity*, 14th ed. New York: McGraw-Hill.

Kulick, Don. 2009. "Can There Be an Anthropology of Homophobia?" In *Homophobias: Lust and Longing across Space and Time*, edited by David A.B. Murray, 19–33. Durham, NC: Duke University Press. http://dx.doi.org/10.1215/9780822391395-002.

Kuttner, Robert. 2013. "The Debt We Shouldn't Pay: The First 5,000 Years by David Graeber." *The New York Review of Books* 60, no. 8. Available at: http://www.nybooks. com/articles/archives/2013/may/09/debt-we-shouldnt-pay/ (accessed 28 April 2015).

Lakner, Christoph, and Branko Milanovic. 2013. "Global Income Distribution: From the Fall of the Berlin Wall to the Great Recession." World Bank Policy Research Working Paper 6719. http://dx.doi.org/10.1596/1813-9450-6719.

Larsen, Christian Albrekt. 2007. "The Institutional Logic of Welfare Attitudes: How Welfare Regimes Influence Public Support." *Comparative Political Studies* 2007:1–24.

Larsen, Christian Albrekt. 2008. "The Political Logic of Labour Market Reforms and Popular Images of Target Groups." *Journal of European Social Policy* 18 (1): 50–63. http://dx.doi.org/10.1177/0958928707084451.

Lee, Ching Kwan. 2006. "Mapping the Terrain of Chinese Labor Ethnography." In *Working in China: Ethnographies of Labor and Workplace Transformation*, edited by Ching Kwan Lee, 1–12. London: Routledge.

Lee, Ching Kwan, and Mark Selden. 2008. "Inequality and Its Enemies in Revolutionary and Reform China." *Economic and Political Weekly* 43 (52): 27–36.

Lindert, Kathy. 2005. "Brazil: Bolsa Familia Program–Scaling-up Cash Transfers for the Poor." *Managing for Development Results Principles in Action: Sourcebook on Emerging Good Practices*. Washington, DC: World Bank. Available at: http://www.mfdr.org/sourcebook/6-1Brazil-BolsaFamilia.pdf (accessed 29 April 2015).

Lindert, Kathy, Emmanuel Skoufias, and Joseph Shapiro. 2006 "Redistributing Income to the Poor and the Rich: Public Transfers in Latin America and the Caribbean." *Social Safety Nets Primer Series*. Washington, DC: World Bank. Available at: http://siteresources.worldbank.org/SOCIALPROTECTION/Resources/SP-Discussion-papers/Safety-Nets-DP/0605.pdf (accessed 29 April 2015).

Loewenstein, Antony. 2013. *Profits of Doom: How Vulture Capitalism Is Swallowing the World*. Melbourne: Melbourne University Publishing.

Macpherson, Crawford Brough. 1962. *The Political Theory of Possessive Individualism*. Oxford: Clarendon Press.

Marx, Karl. 1891. *Wage Labour and Capital*. Translated by Frederick Engels. Pamphlet. Available at: https://www.marxists.org/archive/marx/works/1847/wage-labour/index.htm (accessed 29 April 2015).

McCall, Leslie. 2001. *Complex Inequality: Gender, Class, and Race in the New Economy*. London: Routledge.

McCloskey, Deirdre N. 2010. *Bourgeois Dignity: Why Economics Can't Explain the Modern World*. Chicago: University of Chicago Press.

McGill, Kenneth. 2009. "The Discursive Construction of the German Welfare State: Interests and Institutionality." *Journal of Linguistic Anthropology* 19 (2): 266–85. http://dx.doi.org/10.1111/j.1548-1395.2009.01034.x.

McKinnon, Susan. 2000. "Domestic Exceptions: Evans-Pritchard and the Creation of Nuer Patrilineality and Equality." *Cultural Anthropology* 15 (1): 35–83. http://dx.doi.org/10.1525/can.2000.15.1.35.

Mintz, Sidney W. 1985. *Sweetness and Power: The Place of Sugar in Modern History*. New York: Viking.

Mintz, Sidney W., and Eric R. Wolf. 1989. "Reply to Michael Taussig." *Critique of Anthropology* 9 (1): 25–31. http://dx.doi.org/10.1177/0308275X8900900103.

Morgen, Sandra, and Jeff Maskovsky. 2003. "The Anthropology of Welfare "Reform": New Perspectives on us Urban Poverty in the Post-Welfare Era." *Annual Review of Anthropology* 32 (1): 315–38. http://dx.doi.org/10.1146/annurev.anthro.32.061002.093431.

Morton, Gregory Duff. 2014. "Protest Before the Protests: The Unheard Politics of a Welfare Panic in Brazil." *Anthropological Quarterly* 87 (3): 925–33. http://dx.doi.org/10.1353/anq.2014.0037.

Nash, June. 2001. *Mayan Visions: The Quest for Autonomy in an Age of Globalization*. London: Routledge.

Nhlapo, Thandabantu. 2000. "The African Customary Law of Marriage and the Rights Conundrum." In *Beyond Rights Talk and Culture Talk: Comparative Essays on the Politics of Rights and Culture*, edited by Mahmood Mamdani, 136–48. London: St. Martin's Press.

Ortiz, Isabel, and Matthew Cummins. 2011. "Global Inequality: Beyond the Bottom Billion–A Rapid Review of Income Distribution in 141 Countries." Unicef Social and Economic Policy Working Paper. http://dx.doi.org/10.2139/ssrn.1805046.

Ortiz, Sutti. 2006. "Decisions and Choices: The Rationality of Economic Actors." In *A Handbook of Economic Anthropology*, 2nd ed., edited by James G. Carrier, 58–75. Cheltenham, UK: Edward Elgar Publishing. http://dx.doi.org/10.4337/97818498092 90.00011.

Ortner, Sherry. 1974. "Is Female to Male as Nature is to Culture?" In *Woman, Culture, and Society*, edited by Michelle Zimbalist Rosaldo, Louise Lamphere, and Joan Bamberger, 67–87. Stanford, CA: Stanford University Press.

Parreñas, Rhacel Salazar. 2001. *Servants of Globalization: Women, Migration and Domestic Work*. Stanford, CA: Stanford University Press.

Parreñas, Rhacel Salazar. 2008. *The Force of Domesticity: Filipina Migrants and Globalization*. New York: NYU Press.

Peebles, Gustav. 2010. "The Anthropology of Credit and Debt." *Annual Review of Anthropology* 39 (1): 225–40. http://dx.doi.org/10.1146/annurev-anthro-090109-133856.

Pels, Peter, and Oscar Salemink. 2000. "Introduction: Locating the Colonial Subjects of Anthropology." In *Colonial Subjects: Essays on the Practical History of Anthropology*, edited by Peter Pels and Oscar Salemink, 1–52. Ann Arbor: University of Michigan Press.

Phelps, Glenn, and Steve Crabtree. 2013. "Worldwide, Median Household Income dbout $10,000." Poll from Gallup, Inc., December 16. Available at: http://www.gallup.com/poll/166211/worldwide-median-household-income-000.aspx (accessed 20 October 2015).

Pieterse, Jan Nederveen. 2009. "Prologue: New Balance." In *Politics of Globalization*, edited by Samir Dasgupta and Jan Nederveen Pieterse, xiii–xxv. New Delhi: SAGE.

Piketty, Thomas. 2014. *Capital in the Twenty-First Century*. Cambridge, MA: Belknap Press. http://dx.doi.org/10.4159/9780674369542.

Piketty, Thomas, and Emmanuel Saez. 2014. "Inequality in the Long Run." *Science* 344 (6186): 838–43. http://dx.doi.org/10.1126/science.1251936.

Povinelli, Elizabeth. 1998. "The State of Shame: Australian Multiculturalism and the Crisis of Indigenous Citizenship." *Critical Inquiry* 24 (2): 575–610. http://dx.doi.org/10.1086/448886.

Povinelli, Elizabeth. 2002. *The Cunning of Recognition: Indigenous Alterities and the Making of Australian Multiculturalism*. Durham, NC: Duke University Press. http://dx.doi.org/10.1215/9780822383673.

Povinelli, Elizabeth A. 2006. *The Empire of Love: Toward a Theory of Intimacy, Genealogy, and Carnality*. Durham, NC: Duke University Press. http://dx.doi.org/10.1215/9780822388487.

Puar, Jasbir. 2011. "Citation and Censorship: The Politics of Talking about the Sexual Politics of Israel." *Feminist Legal Studies* 19 (2): 133–42. http://dx.doi.org/10.1007/s10691-011-9176-3.

Puar, Jasbir K. 2013. "Homonationalism as Assemblage: Viral Travels, Affective Sexualities." *Jindal Global Law Review*. 4: 336–9.

Rawls, John. 1971. *A Theory of Justice*. Cambridge, MA: Belknap Press.

Riles, Annelise. 2004. "Real Time: Unwinding Technocratic and Anthropological Knowledge." *American Ethnologist* 31 (3): 392–405. http://dx.doi.org/10.1525/ae.2004.31.3.392.

Riskin, Carl, Renwei Zhao, and Shi Li. 2001. In *China's Retreat from Equality: Income Distribution and Economic Transition*, edited by Carl Riskin, Renwei Zhao, and Shi Li, 3–22. New York: M.E. Sharpe.

Rodney, Walter. 1974. *How Europe Underdeveloped Africa*. Washington, DC: Howard University Press.

Rosaldo, Michelle Zimbalist, Louise Lamphere, and Joan Bamberger. 1974. "Introduction." In *Woman, Culture, and Society*, edited by Michelle Zimbalist Rosaldo, Louise Lamphere, and Joan Bamberger, 1–15. Stanford, CA: Stanford University Press.

Rose, Sonya O. 1988. "Gender Antagonism and Class Conflict: Exclusionary Strategies of Male Trade Unionists in Nineteenth-Century Britain." *Social History* 13 (2): 191–208. http://dx.doi.org/10.1080/03071028808567710.

Seekings, Jeremy, and Nicoli Nattrass. 2008. *Class, Race, and Inequality in South Africa*. New Haven, CT: Yale University Press.

Sen, Amartya. 1993. "Capability and Well-Being." In *The Quality of Life*, edited by Martha Craven Nussbaum and Amartya Kumar Sen, 30–53. Oxford: Clarendon Press.

Shiller, Robert. 2014. "Israeli Home Prices Look Like a Bubble." *Globes: Israel's Business Arena*, January 27. Online edition.

Sitrin, Marina. 2006. *Horizontalism: Voices of Popular Power in Argentina*. Oakland, CA: AK Press.

Sitrin, Marina, and Dario Azzellini. 2014. *They Can't Represent Us! Reinventing Democracy from Greece to Occupy*. London: Verso Books.

Somers, Margaret R., and Fred Block. 2005. "From Poverty to Perversity: Ideas, Markets, and Institutions over 200 Years of Welfare Debate." *American Sociological Review* 70 (2): 260–87. http://dx.doi.org/10.1177/000312240507000204.

Sorenson, Arne. 2013. "US Travel Industry Supports Immigration Reform." *Washington Post*, February 8. Online edition.

Spangler, Sydney A. 2011. "'To Open Oneself Is a Poor Woman's Trouble': Embodied Inequality and Childbirth in South-Central Tanzania." *Medical Anthropology Quarterly* 25 (4): 479–98. http://dx.doi.org/10.1111/j.1548-1387.2011.01181.x.

Spangler, Sydney A., Danika Barry, and Lynn Sibley. 2014. "An Evaluation of Equitable Access to a Community-Based Maternal and Newborn Health Program in Rural Ethiopia." *Journal of Midwifery & Women's Health* 59 (s1): S101–09. http://dx.doi.org/10.1111/jmwh.12133.

Steger, Manfred B. 2003. *Globalization: A Very Short Introduction*. Oxford: Oxford University Press.

Stiglitz, Joseph E. 2014. "On the Wrong Side of Globalization." *New York Times*, March 15. Online edition.

Stocking, George. 1991. "Colonial Situations." In *Colonial Situations: Essays on the Contextualization of Ethnographic Knowledge*, edited by George Stocking, 3–8. Madison: University of Wisconsin Press.

118

Stoler, Ann Laura. 1995. *Race and the Education of Desire: Foucault's History of Sexuality and the Colonial Order of Things*. Durham, NC: Duke University Press.

Sumner, Andy. 2010. "Global Poverty and the New Bottom Billion: What If Three-quarters of the World's Poor Live in Middle-Income Countries?" *IDS Working Papers* 2010 (349): 1–43. http://dx.doi.org/10.1111/j.2040-0209.2010.00349_2.x.

Taussig, Michael. 1980. *The Devil and Commodity Fetishism in South America*. Chapel Hill: University of North Carolina Press.

Taussig, Michael. 1989. "History as Commodity: In Some Recent American (Anthropological) Literature." *Critique of Anthropology* 9 (1): 7–23. http://dx.doi.org/10.1177/0308275X8900900102.

The Take. 2004. Documentary film by Naomi Klein and Avi Lewis. First Run Features/Icarus Films.

Trouillot, Michel-Rolph. 2003. *Global Transformations: Anthropology and the Modern World*. London: Palgrave Macmillan.

Tsing, Anna Lowenhaupt. 2005. *Friction: An Ethnography of Global Connections*. Princeton, NJ: Princeton University Press.

United Nations Development Programme. 2010. *The Real Wealth of Nations: Pathways to Human Development*. Human Development Report, 2010. New York: UNDP.

Wade, Robert H. 2006. "Should We Worry about Income Inequality?" In *Global Inequality: Patterns and Explanations*, edited by David Held and Ayse Kaya, 104–31. London: Polity. http://dx.doi.org/10.2190/EHYF-NEPR-LP0Y-970K.

Wainwright, Hilary. 2003. *Reclaim the State: Experiments in Popular Democracy*. London: Verso.

Walby, Sylvia. 1986. *Patriarchy at Work: Patriarchal and Capitalist Relations in Employment, 1800–1984*. Minneapolis: University of Minnesota Press.

Walby, Sylvia. 2007. "Complexity Theory, Systems Theory, and Multiple Intersecting Social Inequalities." *Philosophy of the Social Sciences* 37 (4): 449–70. http://dx.doi.org/10.1177/0048393107307663.

Wallerstein, Immanuel Maurice. 2004. *World-Systems Analysis: An Introduction*. Durham, NC: Duke University Press.

Weiss, Hadas. 2014. "Homeownership in Israel: The Social Costs of Middle-Class Debt." *Cultural Anthropology* 29 (1): 128–49. http://dx.doi.org/10.14506/ca29.1.08.

Wilkinson, Richard, and Kate Pickett. 2011. *The Spirit Level: Why Greater Equality Makes Societies Stronger*. New York: Bloomsbury.

Wolf, Eric. 1997. *Europe and the People Without History*. Berkeley: University of California Press.

Xin, Tong. 2008. "Women's Labor Activism in China." *Signs: Journal of Women in Culture and Society* 33 (3): 515–18.

Xingdou, Hu. 2009. "China's Poor: Always with Us?" *Open Democracy*, November 5. Available at: https://www.opendemocracy.net/openeconomy/hu-xingdou/chinas-poor-always-with-us (accessed 29 April 2015).

Yamabhai, Inthira, Adun Mohara, Sripen Tantivess, Kakanang Chaisiri, and Yot Teerawattananon. 2011. "Government Use Licenses in Thailand: An Assessment of the Health and Economic Impacts." *Globalization and Health* 7 (28): 131–49.

119

INDEX

and labor, 49
See also indigenous peoples
ethnography
elite people and institutions, 29–30
ethnic stereotypes, 8
and globalization, 3–4, 24–26, 30–33
high schools in USA, 90–92
and inequality, 3, 4, 24–26, 101–2
lack in anthropological work, 22–23
and welfare, 72
See also anthropology
European Union (EU), 52n1
Evans-Pritchard, E.E., 10–11, 92, 93
equality in societies, 10–11
on witchcraft, 92, 93

F
factories, 78–82, 84–85
Fallers, Lloyd, 2
Ferguson, James, 39
Filipina women, 43–44
Fischer, Edward F., relationships in anthropology, 29
forced labor, 16–17
Fox Piven, Frances, 70
Freedom Charter (South Africa), 66–67
Freeman, Carla, gender discrimination, 44, 49
free trade, and economic inequality, 17, 30–33
Friedman, Eli, 80
Friends of Gongchao, 82

G
garment industry, 49
gay rights, 50
Geertz, Clifford, on economic divisions, 9
gender
discrimination, 42–44, 49
and economic inequality, 13, 41
and globalization, 42–43
inequality in Kewa people, 12–13
local and global concerns, 42–44
plastic surgery and beauty, 96–97
and production of inequality, 41–44
as systematic inequality, 5–6
Geschiere, Peter, Maka people and witchcraft, 93–94
Gini coefficient, 27
Glendale (South Africa), 68–70
global income, 27–28, 36–37

global inequality
and anthropology, 28–30
as approach, 1–2, 4–6
and culture, 30
distribution and statistics, 27–28
emergence, 16–17
and institutions, 5–6, 30
vs. local, 1–2, 3–4, 24–26
global institutions. *See* institutions
globalization
anthropology and ethnography, 3–4, 24–26, 30–33
definitions, 2
economy and economic integration, 17–20
gender discrimination, 42–43
and nation-states, 52–54
starting point, 15
winners, 77
Gonzales, Roberto G., undocumented workers, 61–62
Graeber, David, on debt, 34–35
Gupta, Akhil, 39

H
Hacker, Jacob S., on democracy, 48
Hairong, Yan, worker resistance in China, 80, 81
harmonization of trade, 31–32
health and health system, 95, 96, 97–99
high schools, and preparation for future, 89–92
Hochschild, Arlie Russell, gender discrimination, 43–44
Holland, Dorothy C., 89
Holmes, Douglas R., relationships and elite, 29
Holston, James, politics and rights, 55–59
homonationalism, 50
homophobia, 6
horizontalidad ("horizontalism"), 82–85
housing protests, 86–87
human development index, 75
human rights, 53–54
Hutchinson, Sharon Elaine, equality and stratification, 10–11

I
Ibhawoh, Bonny, 54
illegal citizens, USA, 59–63

124

and labor, 68, 71
nation-states, 65–66, 68–70
perversity thesis and morality of
recipients, 70–72
poverty and redistribution, 73–76
terminology in, 72–73
Wilkinson, Richard G., on well-being,
98–99
Wilton Burnham High School (Ohio),
90–91
witchcraft and sorcery, 92–95
Wolf, Eric, history and economy, 21–22, 24
Wolf, Martin, poor countries and
globalization, 39–40
women
childbirth and exclusion, 98
discrimination, 12–13, 42–43, 49
See also gender

workers
discipline, 36–37
domestic workers, 43–44
ethnic discrimination, 49
migration, 43–44, 61, 78–80
social action, 78–82, 84–85
students as, 91
undocumented, 60–63
See also labor
world system, 18, 21–24
World Trade Organization (WTO),
30–31

Y
youth, undocumented, 61–62

Z
Zapatista movement and EZLN, 25

127